MEMORY POWER

Memory-boosting puzzles & facts to improve your memory

Michael Powell

Bath · New York · Cologne · Melbourne · Delhi
Hong Kong · Shenzhen · Singapore · Amsterdam

This edition published by Parragon Books Ltd in 2014 and distributed by

Parragon Inc.
440 Park Avenue South, 13th Floor
New York, NY 10016
www.parragon.com

Copyright © Parragon Books Ltd 2014

Arrangement copyright © Susanna Geoghegan
Packaged by Susanna Geoghegan
Cover design by Talking Design
Inside designed by Bag of Badgers and Angela Wilkinson

ISBN: 978-1-4723-6424-1

Printed in China

CONTENTS

INTRODUCTION

IT IS MEMORY THAT DEFINES US, MEMORY THAT GROUNDS US AND GUIDES US. IT IS THE CORE OF OUR IDENTITY AND PLAYS A CENTRAL ROLE IN EVERY ASPECT OF OUR LIVES. IT INFORMS WHO WE HAVE BEEN AND WHAT WE WANT TO BECOME. MEMORY IS THE BASIS OF LOVE, FRIENDSHIP, THINKING, LEARNING, AND CREATING. A LIFE WITHOUT MEMORY IS MERELY AN EXISTENCE.

But you could still do with a better one, right? Do those tip-of-the-tongue moments come a little too often? Do you find it hard to concentrate when you have to study for a test? Do you struggle to put a name to a face, or have to write an order list when ordering a round of drinks? Are you worried that your memory will keep on getting worse as you grow older?

You're not alone. But do you think it's possible to train memory? If so, do you believe long-term memory has a limited storage capacity or is limitless?

Fortunately, memory science places no limitation on the capacity of memory because brains are spectacularly plastic, meaning they continue to develop throughout our lives. The functional restructuring of brain cells means that it's never too late to learn new information, change your thought processes, and boost your memory.

The human brain is so big and nutrient hungry that an estimated 25 percent of all our energy expenditure is used to power its 85 billion neurons; new connections are formed between them every time you make a memory. All this brain size and flexibility is fantastic news for those who recognize the importance of good brain health, stimulation, and development. Did you know that the hippocampus—a region of the brain associated with the consolidation of information from short-term to long-term memory, and spatial navigation—continues to grow new brain cells well into old age?

This book is a straightforward guide to improving your memory and actually growing your brain. It's a neurogenetic memory system made up of a wide range of puzzles, quizzes, and challenges designed for performing different memory tasks to give you a focused workout. The target areas are nutrition, attention, concentration, visual, auditory, kinesthetic, spatial, musical, intuitive, deliberate practice, and more than a dozen powerful mnemonic techniques.

The first half explains how the memory works and details the major different types that form a complex memory matrix. The second half introduces you to lots of strategies and tips that will expand your memory capacity.

Currently, some of the world's top memory athletes can recite the first 65,000 digits of Pi or memorize 60 shuffled packs of playing cards after viewing them only once. None of them were born with this ability. They use memory techniques and have spent years practicing. You, too, can improve your memory. There's no secret. You don't have to be a genius. You just need a few techniques and you will start to see results within hours. Even now, you remember more than you think, and often failures of memory are caused by a simple lack of attention.

If you are serious about improving your memory you should read this book cover to cover. But if you want to focus on specific issues, you can dip in and out as you please since most of the topics are self-contained, although some of them refer back to earlier sections. Say no to memory decline, read on and start to become more productive today!

LIFE IS A ROUGH BIOGRAPHY. MEMORIES SMOOTH OUT THE EDGES.

(TERRI GUILLEMETS)

HOW THE BRAIN
REMEMBERS

WHO DOESN'T WISH THEY HAD A BETTER MEMORY?
BUT FEW OF US HAVE THE FIRST CLUE HOW OUR
MEMORIES WORK. SOME PEOPLE SHRUG OFF
MEMORY LAPSES, BELIEVING THAT THEY HAVE
ALWAYS BEEN FORGETFUL, OR VIEWING THEM AS
AN INEVITABLE CONSEQUENCE OF ADVANCING
YEARS. NEITHER NEED APPLY TO YOU.

When an individual pops up on television making claims of photographic (eidetic) memory, we blindly admire their miraculous mind powers. However, the good news is that genuine eidetic memory—the ability to recall events, images, or other data with almost perfect precision—is very rare. It's more common in early childhood, but the majority of the extraordinary memory feats displayed by adults are the result of sophisticated memory techniques collectively referred to as mnemonics. Anyone can learn these systems with practice, regardless of their intelligence.

We can all transform our memory powers and it starts by learning how the brain remembers. In the past, memory was compared to a filing cabinet; next, our memories were increasingly likened to a hard drive, which is a terrible comparison because computers store information randomly. Today neuroscientists believe that memory is much more tangled and complex, involving the interaction of many different sensory and memory systems across the entire brain.

The memory-forming process begins with perception. We see, hear, feel, touch, and smell, and the resulting electrochemical impulses travel to a part of the brain called the hippocampus (the name comes from the ancient Greek for horse—*hippos*—and sea monster—*kampos*—as its appearance is similar to a seahorse). This filters out and simplifies the data and integrates all the sensory information into one combined package. The hippocampus and the frontal cortex of the brain are involved in deciding what information is worth remembering.

STUDY THE PICTURE FOR TWO MINUTES. LOOK AT IT CAREFULLY AND TRY TO REMEMBER AS MANY DETAILS AS POSSIBLE. AFTER THE TIME IS UP, TURN THE PAGE AND ANSWER THE QUESTIONS.

1. What color is the balloon?

2. How many butterflies are there?

3. What is directly to the left of the handprint?

4. What animal was asleep on the armchair?

5. What object is directly below the hat?

6. Are the stripes on the cushion vertical or horizontal?

7. Does the stalk of the leaf point to the right or left?

8. What object is in the top right-hand corner?

9. Is the envelope open or closed?

10. What does the Polaroid photo show?

11. How many colors does the knitted hat have?

12. Is the apple closest to the hat or the shell?

13. Which three objects are not in the picture: rope, pencils, sock, key, lollipop, bell, sunglasses, beans, bow tie?

14. Name three metal objects.

15. How many hats are there?

16. What color of paint is on the paintbrush?

17. Which two objects are NOT in the picture?

18. How many pairs of shoes are there?

19. What sport could you play with the ball?

20. What flower was on the bottom line?

Now check your answers by looking at page 7, then *see* page 142 for your assessment.

Your brain has about 100 billion cells called neurons which receive and transmit electro-chemical signals. Neurons communicate with each other in response to the stimuli that your senses receive, and memories are laid down as these connections are reinforced by repetition, in much the same way that cross-country skiers create grooves in the snow, which make a route easier to traverse.

Recent research into gamma waves at the Kavli Institute for Systems Neuroscience and Centre for the Biology of Memory at the Norwegian University of Science and Technology (NTNU) has shown that brain cells also use a switching system to literally tune into the wavelength of other neurons; they can choose which of the thousands of inputs to focus on, by tuning into different gamma wavelengths, like turning the dial on a radio.

Study this picture for one minute. Pay particular attention to the food items and try to remember as many details about them as possible. After the minute is up, turn the page, keep reading, and then answer the two questions.

The more you learn, the more of these connections are created between neurons. These fluid connections are changing and developing all the time. Connections which are used very little will disintegrate while those that are reinforced grow stronger, which is why we learn by practice and forget or lose specialized skills through disuse. For instance, it is widely acknowledged that during infanthood there is a critical period for the acquisition of certain skills, such as native language. A young child has heightened sensitivity to learning languages but after the age of about five, native-like fluency becomes progressively challenging because the brain becomes more specialized, and any unused linguistic neural pathways are appropriated for other salient brain functions.

To commit something to memory you must first pay attention. The sensory information enters your short-term memory. It can keep between four and seven items for about 30 seconds (this increases if you use a technique such as chunking—*see* page 79—to break down a set, such as twelve numbers chunked into three groups of four). You can also increase this time by repeating words to yourself, effectively resubmitting the information to your short-term memory.

Important information that you (and/or your subconscious) deem worthy of remembering, passes from your short-term memory into your long-term memory through repetition, emotional engagement, and your existing network of memory associations (since the more you know about a subject, the easier it is to make meaningful and memorable associations and neural connections).

In the previous exercise you may have noticed that you were only able to retain certain details if you made a specific point of noticing them, while other information was available to you with some prompting, although you may not have recalled it if you had merely listed everything. Notice, too, that third-party suggestion can alter your memories (did questions 12 and 17 implant the false memory of an apple?).

So, here are your two questions:

1. Write down all the food items that you can remember.

2. Write down all the nonfood items that you can remember.

Unsurprisingly, we remember information better when we pay special attention to it. This is blindingly obvious, but it also highlights that sometimes we pay attention to the wrong things and then think that we have a bad memory when we can't recall the desired information. You were instructed to focus on the food items; since you had limited time it was inevitable that your recall of the other items was more limited. You no doubt counted the slices of bread, noticed that there were four apples, one of which had been eaten; you counted three eggs and four bread rolls. Maybe you even had time to observe how the apples were arranged—was it A or B? Go back and check!

A   B

So you've learned the importance of focus, but now you're feeling cheated. So here are five more questions.

1. What color is the memory stick?

2. What color is the rubber band on the rolled-up wad of bills?

3. What color is the single rose?

4. What color is the iron?

5. What color is the telephone?

Sorry, you're not getting rewarded that easily. That was another opportunity to ram home the message that attention is everything. If you had been asked to focus on the colors red and black, these five answers would be so easy you'd be complaining.

The best way to improve recall is to increase attention at the memory-forming stage. Most memory recall problems are actually caused by a failure to store information properly in the first place. Most of the strategies in this book enhance this memory-forming stage.

So memory creation requires attention, but memory *retrieval* can be conscious or involuntary (for example, a piece of music or a smell can make you recall an incident from years ago). The stronger your network of associations, the easier your recall will be, even if you have to approach a memory from an oblique angle (a technique called memory priming, which involves brainstorming your memory for everything you know on a subject to supply the answer that eludes you—*see* page 47).

Another way to categorize long-term memory is the distinction between declarative and nondeclarative (procedural) memory. Declarative memory (*see* page 45) is information we consciously store, such as facts and events, and we tend to describe and think about them using words; procedural memory (*see* page 49) involves actions—often but not exclusively physical—that we perform without having any conscious awareness of how we learned them or any need to consciously recall them: these include walking, talking, riding a bicycle, taking a shower, catching a ball. These long-term memories automatically snap into action whenever we need them.

Another important feature of memory is that it is fluid. Memories are continually being modified to inform our present circumstances. Every time we access a memory, we reinforce but also subtly change it, depending on our current interpretation. Recent research by Northwestern Medicine, published in the *Journal of Neuroscience* in August 2012, indicates that recalling a memory can make it less accurate. Lead researcher of the study, Donna Bridge, explains: "A memory is not simply an image produced by time traveling back to the original event—it can be an image that is somewhat distorted because of the prior times you remembered it". In fact, your memory can grow less precise with each recall by reinforcing earlier recall errors, so that it can end up totally false. This helps to explain why revisiting a cherished place from our past sometimes fails to live up to expectations because we have idealized it by repeated recall.

GRID MEMORY EXERCISE

This exercise extends over three days. Turn over now to receive your instructions.

DAY 1:

Spend two minutes studying the 25 objects on the previous page. Do not read any farther until you have done this.

WELCOME BACK

In the Northwestern Medicine study in Chicago, subjects had to memorize the location of a group of objects and then place them in a grid, from memory, three times over the next three days. The study found that inaccuracies in recall from the second day negatively affected recall on the third day. This is why it is important when learning, to return regularly to the source material rather than entrench inaccurate memories (if you have ever had to learn lines for a play, you will be familiar with how easy it is to learn—and how hard it is to unlearn—faulty approximations and wrong words).

Now draw a 5 x 6 grid on another piece of paper. Referring to the words only, try to place each item on your blank grid. Do not check your answers.

apple, croissant, laptop, shirt, green iron, starfish, hand with note, chick, nut, chair, crossed stack of bills, red balloon, red iron, stereo, side view notes, notepad, cat, shoes, telephone, guinea pig, calculator, cup and saucer, laptop, sunglasses, green balloon

DAY 2:

Do not look at the images or your grid from Day 1. Referring to the words only, try to place each item on another blank grid. Do not check your answers.

DAY 3:

Do not look at the images or your grids from Day 1 or 2. Referring to the words only, try to place each item on another blank grid.

Now check your answers from all three days and you'll be able to observe and track the compounded recall errors you have made throughout the exercise.

MYTHS ABOUT MEMORY

It's curious that there are so many persistent myths about memory, despite the fact that we all use and experience our own memories every day. Here are 12 common misconceptions:

MYTH 1—AMNESIACS FORGET WHO THEY ARE

By far the most common type of amnesia is anterograde amnesia, the inability to form new memories; retrograde amnesia, the loss of past memories and identity, is much rarer. Despite this, retrograde amnesiacs are over-represented in movies—probably because they make a better plot.

MYTH 2—MEMORY IS A THING

Many people view memory as an innate quality located in a specific part of the brain, or as separate items stored ready for retrieval. Although certain parts of the brain play important roles in memory function, memory is a holistic multifaceted process rather than a physical place; it is an activity and a skill that can be developed with practice and using strategies. Also, no memories exist in isolation; they exist in a matrix of associations.

MYTH 3—SOME PEOPLE REMEMBER BEING BORN

It is highly unlikely that an adult can recall episodic memories from the first year of life, mainly because the hippocampus is too immature to form and store long-lasting memories.

MYTH 4—HYPNOSIS CAN HELP WITNESSES OF CRIMES TO RECALL MORE ACCURATE DETAILS

Hypnosis can lead to more recall but not always greater accuracy; sometimes it can reinforce inaccurate memories and create false ones. In fact, it is easy to create false memories even without hypnosis, as several "familial informant false narrative procedure" studies have shown. Parents are encouraged to mislead their grown-up children by introducing a false memory into a childhood reminiscing exercise. Afterward, up to 30 percent of the students recall the false event as if it had really happened.

FALSE MEMORY EXERCISE

One of the most interesting things about memory is how easily it can be distorted. This exercise demonstrates how simple it is to implant a false memory.

Ask a friend to perform a short memory test with you. Prepare them for the test by saying the following sentence:

"I am going to say a list of words that I want you to try to remember. Pay attention to me carefully while I read out this list. Make a mental note of them and try to remember them. Are you ready? The list begins now."

Read out this list of 15 words, allowing about a second for each word.

Cotton candy, sugar, bitter, love, taste, bite, honey, nice, tooth, pastry, chocolate, heart, cake, eat, pie

Now say: *"OK, that's the list. Now spend a few moments with your thoughts while you try to remember as many items on the list as you can."*

Hand them pen and paper and get them to write down as many of the words as they can.

Now say: *"I'd like you to tell me whether these four words were on the list. The first word is taste. Write down yes, no, or not sure. Was taste on the list? The second word is roof. Was that one of the words on my list? Write down yes, no, or not sure. The third word is brief. Write down yes, no, or not sure. Did brief appear on my list? The fourth word is sweet. Did sweet appear on my list? Write down yes, no, or not sure. OK, the memory test is over. Now tell me: what did you write for sweet?"*

Most people who take this memory test are convinced that "sweet" is on the list. However, most of the words are related to sweet. In this instance the false memory was created by association and the power of suggestion.

STUDY THIS PICTURE FOR ONE MINUTE. AFTER THE MINUTE IS UP, TURN THE PAGE, STUDY THE SECOND PICTURE, AND ANSWER THE QUESTION.

TEN ITEMS ARE MISSING FROM THIS PICTURE.
HOW MANY OF THEM CAN YOU WRITE DOWN?

MYTH 5—OLDER PEOPLE HAVE POOR MEMORIES

It is well established that mental exercises during childhood and late adulthood contribute to a slower mental decline in old age, but a team at Tübingen University in Germany has proposed a theory that healthy old people don't suffer mental decline at all: they just know so much that their brains take longer to process all the information, in the same way that a computer's hard drive slows down when it's full. It's never too late to develop your memory skills.

MYTH 6—A STRONG MEMORY IS A SIGN OF INTELLIGENCE

Visual working memory capacity has been correlated with academic success and fluid intelligence (problem solving), but having a wide general knowledge, winning quizzes, and peppering your conversation with pithy quotations is no indicator of a high IQ, although it often passes for such. Real intelligence is demonstrated by a person's ability to assimilate new information and to think creatively. However, that is not to say that people who demonstrate extraordinary memory skills lack intelligence, because it takes intelligence and discipline to develop any skill to a high level. If you develop your memory skills, you will be able to outperform a high-IQ person who lacks a systematic approach to memorizing and retrieving information.

MYTH 7—FORGETTING OCCURS GRADUALLY

Actually, most forgetting occurs immediately after an event. Most of what we forget, we never remembered in the first place, or stored in a haphazard way, making retrieval difficult.

MYTH 8—CONFIDENT RECOLLECTIONS ARE
ACCURATE RECOLLECTIONS

Confidence is not an indicator of objectivity nor accuracy of recollection. Our memories are altered by many factors, especially information we receive after the event. Much research has been done on the "misinformation effect" which happens when our episodic memory becomes distorted by post-event information. In one famous study, subjects were shown photos of a college student in a bookstore with different objects; when they were made to read a misleading passage of text after viewing the images, their recall of the objects was adversely affected.

MYTH 9 – DEVELOPING MEMORY SKILLS IS EASY

Anyone can improve their memory, but many of the techniques take practice, just like any other skill. You can learn a mnemonic to memorize the colors of the spectrum but remembering takes effort to learn and apply memory techniques, rather than tricks. Anything worth doing requires attention and mental effort.

MYTH 10 – MEMORY IS LIKE A VIDEO RECORDER

A video recording is an objective and accurate record of visual data, whereas memory is fluid, active, and subjective; memories change every time we access them, which is good for those who want to heal themselves by reframing painful memories, but bad news for the justice system, because the memories of eyewitnesses are notoriously subjective and fickle. We see and remember what our emotions, prejudices, and belief systems want us to remember.

MYTH 11 – MEMORY IS PRIMARILY VISUAL

Memory begins with perception through the five senses, but images stored in the long-term visual memory are reinforced and given meaning by their connection with other stored knowledge, which is often semantic. Researchers at MIT and Harvard demonstrated this with experiments in which participants were shown a stream of 3,000 images of different scenes, such as golf courses, amusement parks, and ocean waves; then they were shown 200 pairs of images, each featuring one previously seen and one new image, and had to pick out the former. Recall was most accurate where the new and old images featured different scenes (e.g. golf course/airport rather than airport/airport), suggesting that during the memorization process, the visual images had been categorized and meaning had been attached to them using a non-visual format.

MYTH 12 – TAKING A PHOTOGRAPH AIDS MEMORY

Actually the opposite is true. A study led by Linda Henkel, a psychology professor at Fairfield University in Connecticut, found that people remember 10 percent fewer objects and 12 percent fewer details than people who just observe them. She explains, "When you press click on that button for the camera, you're sending a signal to your brain saying, 'I've just outsourced this, the camera is going to remember this for me.'" This is further proof that attention is a key component of memory.

PARTY PEOPLE MEMORY TEST

You have thrown a party and these are the first nine people to arrive. They are very pleased to see you. To help you remember who came to your party, use a real camera or your mobile phone to photograph them, either one by one or in small groups—they have held a pose for you. You have just 60 seconds to do this, under 7 seconds for each guest.

CAN YOU PICK OUT YOUR NINE GUESTS FROM THIS IDENTITY PARADE?

NOW TRY THE SAME EXERCISE WITH THIS NEW GROUP OF FRIENDS, ONLY THIS TIME SPEND YOUR 60 SECONDS JUST LOOKING AT THE PEOPLE.

CAN YOU PICK OUT YOUR NINE GUESTS FROM THIS IDENTITY PARADE? YOU SHOULD FIND IT EASIER THIS TIME.

YOU REMEMBER MORE
THAN YOU THINK

In 1946, the American pediatrician Dr. Benjamin Spock published his book *Baby and Child Care*, which went on to become one of the biggest bestsellers of all time. For 50 years its sales were second only to the Bible. Spock encouraged parents to be more flexible and affectionate toward their children and to trust their own parental instincts. His critics blamed him for creating a new permissiveness, a "Spock generation" of pampered and indulged beatniks who sought instant gratification. However, the book's opening sentence and core message, "You know more than you think you do," is very relevant to the study of memory.

We do not remember facts in isolation; everything is connected and context is very important. Here are five images of a reasonably well-known country.

Stripped of context and rotated 180 degrees, the first image is fiendishly elusive for obvious reasons. If you are very familiar with the shape of the country, you might be able to recognize it from the second image without the added context supplied in the third image (that it's an island). Now you simply have to trawl your memory for islands. The fourth image tells you that it is off the coast of Africa (if you know that Mozambique is in Africa). For many people the fifth image supplies enough information to correctly name the island nation. The more context that is supplied, the easier it is to recall the desired information from your memory. The shape becomes familiar when we are supplied with context.

However, if you are still struggling, it is also the name of a 2005 computer-animated comedy movie produced by DreamWorks Animation featuring Marty the zebra (Chris Rock), Alex the lion (Ben Stiller), Melman the giraffe (David Schwimmer), and Gloria the hippopotamus (Jada Pinkett Smith). You see? You remember more than you think. If you are still clueless, then take comfort from the fact that you probably recognize the word "Madagascar" even if you didn't know where it is. Failing that, stored in your memory is, at the very least, the knowledge that "Madagascar" is a country/island/place/movie/name/word.

For decades, cognitive psychologists have believed that although the short-term memory contains fewer items than long-term memory, it is more detailed than the information contained in the long-term memory, which is more generalized and fuzzy. However, recent research by Timothy F. Brady, a cognitive neuroscientist at the Massachusetts Institute of Technology, indicates that long-term memory is capable of retaining much finer visual detail than once thought. Observers were shown 2,500 pictures of real world objects for 3 seconds each over a period of five hours. Later that day they were shown pairs of similar items and asked to choose which of the items they had already seen. Not only were they more than 90 percent correct at identifying familiar items, but they were able to notice subtle differences between two superficially similar objects, such as bells with different handles or differently shaped pieces of fruit.

Here are five images of Madagascar. Only one of them is correct. Can you remember which it is?

See? You do remember more than you think.

SET A TIMER AND ALLOW YOURSELF 90 SECONDS TO OBSERVE THESE OBJECTS. THEN TURN THE PAGE AND FOLLOW THE INSTRUCTIONS.

HERE ARE 20 PAIRS OF OBJECTS. CHOOSE WHICH ITEM FROM EACH PAIR APPEARS ON THE PREVIOUS PAGE.

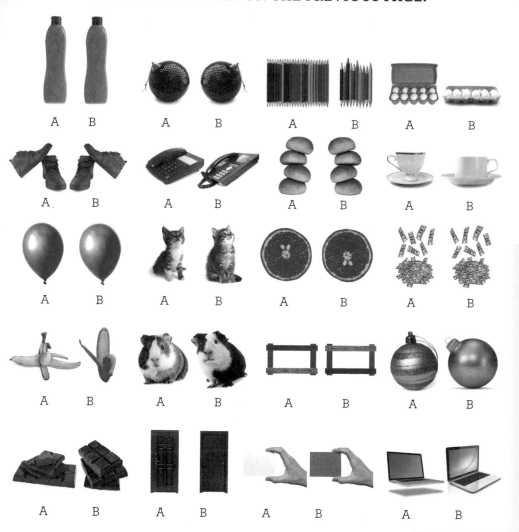

Now check your answers and you may be pleasantly suprised.
Most people will get at least 14 correct.

28

MEMORY ABILITY IS DEVELOPED,
NOT INNATE

A HUNDRED YEARS AGO IT WAS WIDELY
BELIEVED THAT EXPERTS WERE BLESSED WITH
AN INNATE AND SUPERIOR ABILITY TO STORE
INFORMATION IN THEIR MEMORY.

However, recent research has shown that experts develop memory skills that are limited to their specific area of expertise and that their memories are comparable to those of the general public when the same information is presented in an unfamiliar way.

For example, chess grandmasters can recognize a huge number of chess positions and develop optimal moves from them; they can look at a board containing 20 or more chess pieces and remember the positions of each piece. However, if these pieces are randomly arranged rather than replicating actual game play, chess experts fare no better than anyone else. This was demonstrated by a famous study by William Chase and Herbert Simon called "Perception in Chess" which was published in *Cognitive Psychology* in 1973.

This shows that chess experts do not use eidetic (photographic) memory, but instead recall a collection of meaningful associations between the pieces.

Professional mnemonists, like eight-time World Memory Champion Dominic O'Brien, make their living by memorizing vast amounts of data such as decks of cards, lists of numbers, or unfamiliar names. In common with chess experts, they have spent many years of intense preparation developing memory techniques for specific memory tasks. In May 2002, Dominic O'Brien entered the *Guinness Book of Records* for memorizing a random sequence of 2,808 playing cards (54 packs) after looking at each card only once. He then recited them in order and made only eight errors, four of which he corrected. But he, like everyone else in the mnemonist community, has developed a personal system (The Mnemonic Dominic System) and has spent years practicing to reach an international level of performance. If you passionately want to improve your memory, then your innate memory ability is far less important than your willingness to learn and practice the techniques that will show dramatic results.

HOW AND WHY
DO WE FORGET?

To many people, forgetting is an inconvenience with entirely negative consequences, but actually, sifting, refining, and forgetting experiences are important components of the memory process, and forgetting is part of a healthy mind. There are four main reasons why we forget information: storage failure, retrieval failure, interference, and motivation.

STORAGE FAILURE

We often mistakenly talk about having forgotten something when we simply failed to commit it to long-term memory in the first place. Most forgetting takes place soon after we learn something. Our brains decide what information is useful for our day-to-day life, and extraneous data is rejected.

In a famous experiment by research psychologists Raymond Nickerson and Marilyn Adams in 1979, subjects had to pick out a genuine 1-cent coin from 14 inaccurate ones. Fewer than half of the test subjects could identify the correct penny. How could such a seemingly familiar object, handled every day by hundreds of millions of people, be so hard to spot? The reason is that memory is regulated on a need-to-know basis. All that daily life needs is recognizing a penny by its size, shape, color, and a few salient details, such as Lincoln's head. For most people, any deeper knowledge is not needed beyond this basic functional information, so it isn't remembered.

Try this experiment now. Think about your front door key. How much detail can you remember? Shape, size, and color most likely, enough so you can tell it apart from any other keys on your key ring. But what about the writing? You can probably guess the brand name, but fetch it now and take a look at the other side; there may be a whole load of numbers and writing you've never even noticed before, let alone remembered.

RETRIEVAL FAILURE

"We really construct memories rather than record them," explains Elizabeth Loftus, Professor of Psychology at the University of Washington. "We store bits and pieces of information, and when it comes time to retrieve we take bits and pieces of our experience from different times and we integrate it." Retrieval failure is one of the most common causes of forgetting. The information is in your long-term memory (and you may even know that you know it), but you can't access it. One explanation is "decay theory": that just as we construct memories, we reinforce them by revisiting them; if memories are not revisited, they gradually fade away. However, this clearly doesn't apply to all long-term memories, since we can all recall events, faces, and places that we haven't visited or thought about for decades.

INTERFERENCE

The "interference theory" of memory suggests that memories compete and interfere with each other in two basic ways: proactively (an old memory makes recall of a new memory more difficult) and retroactively (when new information disrupts your ability to recall older information). Much research has been done on the effect of interference on the learning of lists; unsurprisingly, as the number of lists increases, so does the interference. In one such experiment, subjects had to learn a list of ten paired adjectives. Two days later they were able to recall close to 70 percent of the items. However, subjects who were also asked to learn a new list the day after the first recalled only 40 percent, and those who had learned a third list had only 25 percent recall.

MOTIVATION

Sometimes we either suppress (consciously) or repress (subconsciously) memories, often unpleasant and even traumatic events. Psychologists disagree about the mechanism involved in repression, since a major component of memory retention is revisiting and rehearsal of memories, so it may simply be that by avoiding thinking of unpleasant events our memories of them are weakened.

Humans tend to have a greater recall of unpleasant memories compared with positive ones. This psychological phenomenon is called negativity bias. While it is an important survival skill for avoiding danger and minimizing the repetition of negative experiences, research has shown that negative experiences have a greater impact on people than positive or neutral ones. Professor Teresa Amabile is Edsel Bryant Ford Professor of Business Administration in the Entrepreneurial Management Unit at Harvard Business School. Her research into the psychology of everyday worklife has found that professionals viewed negative setbacks twice as strongly as positive achievements in a working day. For this reason, consciously trying to act and think positively is an important tool, because we have to overcompensate for negativity bias.

TAKING CARE OF YOUR HEALTH IS THE
BEST MEMORY BOOST

Memory techniques can produce substantial cognitive improvements, but by far the best way to boost your memory is to improve your health. From exercise to sleep and nutrition, here are some of nature's ways to improve your memory.

SLEEP

Your brain relies on sleep to figure out which neural connections need to be reinforced. It can't do this effectively while you are awake, which is why sleep is essential for memory consolidation and learning new information. Research has shown that depriving students of sleep after they had learned a new skill significantly decreased their memory of that skill up to three days later. Some areas of memory are affected more than others. Procedural memory (which involves motor and perceptual skills—*see* page 49) is more affected by sleep than declarative memory (learning of facts—*see* page 45).

STRESS

Stress interferes with neurotransmitter function and can even decrease the size of the prefrontal cortex and the hippocampus. Neurotoxins such as drugs and alcohol also place considerable stress on your body and nervous system; heavy alcohol use has also been linked to a reduction in the size of the hippocampus. However, moderate drinking appears to be better for your memory than total abstinence.

EXERCISE

Taking moderate exercise at least three times a week increases blood flow and oxygenation of the brain, which improves neural function, including memory. Studies have shown that the speed of declarative memory tasks, such as learning vocabulary words, was increased by 20 percent when performed after an intense workout.

DENTAL HYGIENE

Flossing before bed can boost your memory. When bad bacteria collect between your teeth, they enter the bloodstream and cause inflammation throughout the body, including the brain.

MEMORY FOODS

A healthy diet is vital for good brain function. Don't skip breakfast or cut out food groups. A study at Tufts University found that cutting out carbohydrates impaired performance on memory-based tasks.

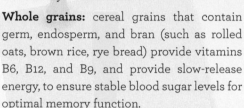

Whole grains: cereal grains that contain germ, endosperm, and bran (such as rolled oats, brown rice, rye bread) provide vitamins B6, B12, and B9, and provide slow-release energy, to ensure stable blood sugar levels for optimal memory function.

Nuts and seeds: these are a powerhouse for the memory and many of them help maintain healthy levels of the calming neurotransmitter serotonin and the mood stabilizing hormones epinephrine, norepinephrine, and dopamine; they also increase oxygen flow to the brain. Many (especially pecans) are a good source of zinc, used in the hippocampus to process memory, provide omega-6 and omega-3 fatty acids, and protect the brain against motor neuron degeneration.

Berries and green vegetables: dark berries such as blueberries, black currants, and blackberries are the best memory fruits; they provide vitamin C and protect the brain from oxidative stress; strawberries contain more vitamin C than oranges and reduce the risk of age-related brain decline; pomegranates and dark leafy green vegetables (spinach, broccoli, kale) contain high levels of folic acid and may promote healthy beta-amyloid function to reduce the risk of Alzheimer's disease.

Avocados: the term "superfood" is much overused, but avocados deserve the accolade; they are rich in monounsaturated fat, which aids blood flow, they lower blood pressure, and stimulate the central nervous system.

Fish: oily fish (salmon, mackerel, tuna) are rich in omega-3 fatty acids, which are very important for the function of neurons.

Sage: this herb has been used as a memory tonic for thousands of years. Many studies have focused on the essential oil but adding fresh sage to your diet may also promote memory.

You can learn heaps of mnemonics and read as many books on the subject as you like, but all that memory-busting work will be wasted unless you fuel your brain and body with the correct nutrients. Here are two practical and tasty ways to help develop optimal brain health.

MEMORY SMOOTHIE

This delicious drink will help to stabilize blood sugar, increase blood flow to the brain, and supply you with phytonutrients, folates, and beta-carotene.

½ cup unsweetened carrot juice

⅔ cup fresh blueberries

½ cup peeled and grated raw beets

¼ cup chopped avocado

heaping ½ cup toasted almonds or walnuts

3 normal size ice cubes

½ tsp. fresh lime juice

1 thin slice fresh ginger

Place all the ingredients in a blender and blend until the texture is smooth and velvety.

POWER SEED AND NUT GRANOLA BARS

2 cups rolled oats

½ cup (1 stick) butter

3 tbsp. flax seeds

¼ cup pecans

3 tbsp. almonds

3 tbsp. shelled sunflower seeds

⅓ cup brown sugar

3 tbsp. golden syrup or honey

1. Preheat the oven to 350°F.
    Place all ingredients in a food processor and pulse until fully mixed. Don't overdo it: you don't want the oats to completely lose their integrity.

2. Spoon the mixture into a lightly greased baking pan, measuring about 8 inches square, and then press the mixture flat.

3. Bake in the preheated oven until golden brown (about 20–30 minutes).

SHORT-TERM MEMORY

SHORT-TERM MEMORY, ALSO KNOWN AS ACTIVE OR PRIMARY MEMORY, INVOLVES TEMPORARY STORAGE OF INFORMATION WHICH DECAYS VERY QUICKLY.

Most of us can reliably store between four and seven items in our short-term memory for between 15 and 30 seconds. Short-term memory is often referred to as working memory, but actually they are different. The short-term memory only stores information, while, as the name suggests, working memory involves mental organization or manipulation of the information, as happens when you perform mental calculations or play tic-tac-toe or chess in your head (depending on your working memory ability).

Your five main senses—sight, hearing, taste, smell, touch—receive sensory information which is briefly stored in your short-term memory, as a mixture of auditory, visual, and semantic information (since we might see an object and then repeat—rehearse—the word in our heads, to store the word in our auditory memory). For more information about the part of the short-term memory we call sensory memory, see page 37.

Only information that is rehearsed and encoded passes from the short-term memory into the long-term memory. If you receive a piece of information and someone immediately distracts you and prevents you from rehearsing it, it will quickly fade from your short-term memory. Much research has been done into the size, duration, and effect of interference on short-term memory.

Psychologist George Miller of Princeton University's Department of Psychology was the first person to measure the capacity of the short-term memory. In 1956 he published his seminal paper, "The Magical Number Seven, Plus or Minus Two: Some Limits on Our Capacity for Processing Information," in *Psychological Review*. The paper introduced the "magic number seven (plus or minus two)", which became widely cited as the number of objects a person can hold in their short-term memory without using rehearsal or special memory techniques. Other studies have shown that people find it easier to remember numbers than letters.

THE BROWN–PETERSON TASK

In 1959, Lloyd and Margaret Peterson conducted an experiment with 24 psychology students at Indiana University to measure the duration of the short-term memory when rehearsal is prevented. The students heard a meaningless consonant trigram, e.g. TDH, then they had to immediately count backward verbally in threes or fours from a specified random number for 3, 6, 9, 12, 15, or 18 seconds. The counting was designed to prevent them from rehearsing the trigram in their memories. Participants were able to recall 80 percent of the trigrams after 3 seconds of counting but this fell to less than 10 percent after 18 seconds of counting.

A second experiment was conducted by John Brown with 48 Indiana University psychology students. The control group of 24 students performed the Peterson experiment but the other 24 participants were allowed to repeat the trigram aloud until they were given the number and had to start counting backward from it. The rehearsal interval was varied, and the study concluded that a longer rehearsal period resulted in greater recall.

You can conduct your own Brown–Peterson Task on a willing volunteer. Here are 48 consonant trigrams.

NRP	SGH	SGN	LWH	DTP	RPJ	CLT	ZHW
DTQ	MPX	BKR	ZKC	KBP	XRN	FPS	NWL
PCW	PYK	MCW	MZQ	LJB	JWF	PBZ	YBV
WNG	LRC	BCX	BQM	KSF	LCV	LPD	BQT
PRK	YCV	TBX	DMB	JYW	KFL	XNZ	MDT
WSD	YFP	HCX	DPW	CNJ	YSP	NQW	MDP

If you make up your own trigrams, be sure to avoid memorable acronyms such as MGM or KFC.

Repeat eight times with six different counting times—3, 6, 9, 12, 15, and 18 seconds—and record the number of letters correctly recalled each time. That should keep you busy!

SENSORY MEMORY

YOUR SHORT-TERM MEMORY IS CONTINUALLY BOMBARDED WITH SENSORY INPUT FROM YOUR FIVE MAIN SENSES—SIGHT, HEARING, TASTE, SMELL, AND TOUCH. EACH SENSE HAS A CORRESPONDING SHORT-TERM MEMORY STORE, BUT THE MOST COMMONLY STUDIED ARE SIGHT (ICONIC), HEARING (ECHOIC), AND TOUCH (HAPTIC).

ICONIC MEMORY

This visual sense memory is very brief: less than 100 milliseconds. If you wave a sparkler in the dark, iconic memory allows you to perceive continuity of movement, so the sparkler will appear to draw lines and shapes, because you visually remember its trajectory. Here's another example of iconic memory:

1. Look at the yellow dot for 15 seconds   2. Now look here

Iconic memory is important for visual continuity but its rapid rate of decay accounts for a much-studied psychological phenomenon called "change blindness." This is the failure to notice a change (even significant differences) in a visual stimulus. Our ability to retain visual information in one glance to the next is actually remarkably limited.

LOOK AT THESE TWO PHOTOGRAPHS. HOW QUICKLY CAN YOU SPOT A SINGLE MAJOR DIFFERENCE?

ECHOIC MEMORY

Scientists disagree about how long this auditory memory lasts: anywhere from one to ten seconds. It is easier for us to remember the sounds that have linguistic meaning for us, such as letters, words, and numbers, because these sounds are already stored in our long-term memory. Adults and children with learning disabilities often have shorter echoic memories, so they have to work harder to understand the spoken word, which is why additional visual input can be useful. Visual stimuli can be scanned by the eye again and again while the brain makes sense of the information, whereas auditory information is usually only supplied once. We all have a preference for either visual, auditory, or kinesthetic learning because we often have one dominant type of memory (iconic, echoic, or haptic) and corresponding learning style (take the test on pages 63-68 to find yours).

ECHOIC MEMORY GAME

Give each player a pen and paper. Here are ten lists of one-syllable words. The first list has just four objects and the last has 13. Read the first list aloud evenly and clearly (it should take about two seconds). As soon as you have finished speaking, players attempt to quickly write down all the objects. Now read the next list at the same pace as the first (it should take about two and a half seconds) and once again, players may start writing as soon as you have finished speaking. By the time you reach the tenth list (which should take about seven seconds) most players will be struggling. The person who correctly writes down the most objects is the winner.

cat, bulb, fish, sky

roof, claw, lamp, cup, bed

pin, tree, hat, spade, coat, gun

heart, spoon, tent, cake, horse, wall, spot

shelf, hedge, mouth, chair, bread, girl, box, pig

ear, class, bird, train, bag, rent, salt, wind, comb

hand, rat, soil, door, night, pen, fox, dirt, egg, hawk

moon, wax, nest, wand, sheep, sword, silk, queen, sand, badge, zoo

throne, meal, base, mint, art, ghost, plate, quilt, edge, match, home, rest

tongue, mind, frog, noise, rice, pest, glove, song, rail, vase, dime, bell, shade

Now, as a brief demonstration of the power of "chunking" (*see* page 79), read out these two lists of 12 words (with the rhythm "dum-di-dum-di-dum-di-dum, dum-dum-dum-dum-dum") and see their recall dramatically improve. (You can also repeat some of the longer lists above and chunk them in the same way.)

ghost, hawk, hand, rent, wind, sheep, spade

bread, home, frog, cake, shelf

----

heart, song, hat, door, tree, sword, ear

sky, glove, hedge, pest, cup

HAPTIC MEMORY

This sensory memory is the information that is briefly retained after a tactile stimulus has been supplied. We have haptic sensory receptors all over our bodies that can detect different types of tactile stimuli, such as pressure, pain, and itching. This information is transmitted through the spinal cord to the primary somatosensory area in the human cortex, which is located in the postcentral gyrus of the parietal lobe of the brain.

Developments in haptic technology have snowballed since the beginning of the twenty-first century so now we are accustomed to receiving haptic feedback from a wide range of everyday consumer devices such as vibrating cell phones, game controllers, and joysticks.

As well as protecting us from danger, information derived from haptic memory enables us to predict how much force to use for everyday tasks, such as grasping and lifting. However, we also use a lot of visual clues, which can sometimes mislead. If identical weights are placed inside two boxes of differing sizes, the smaller box will feel heavier than the bigger one. This is called the Charpentier Illusion, named after the nineteenth-century French physician Augustin Charpentier. The same effect also occurs with construction materials: metal containers and darker objects feel lighter than wooden boxes and brighter objects of the same size and mass. Scientists disagree on the reason why this happens, but it is likely that one factor is a temporary conflict between the visual and haptic memory systems.

TWO SUITCASES TRICK

We have all felt foolish after using too little or too much force to lift a suitcase. You can actually study this phenomenon yourself. Take two identical suitcases. Fill the first so that it is heavy and leave the other one empty. Now ask an unsuspecting victim to help you carry them. Give them the heavy suitcase, so they form a haptic memory of the force required; then a bit later get them to pick up the empty one.

It's really hard to play this trick on yourself because even if you get someone to shuffle the suitcases behind your back, when you pick them up, you will find that your body is primed for both possible outcomes.

LONG-TERM MEMORY

ONCE A MEMORY HAS PASSED FROM THE SHORT-TERM MEMORY BUFFER INTO THE LONG-TERM MEMORY, THE MORE IT IS SUBSEQUENTLY REVISITED AND REHEARSED, THE STRONGER IT BECOMES.

Once implanted, a long-term memory can last forever, but the data isn't fixed in the memory like an insect in amber. Each time a memory is revisited it is altered. This description is the standard Atkinson–Shiffrin Memory Model (formulated in the 1960s by Richard C. Atkinson and Richard Shiffrin) but there are alternative memory models like the Baddeley–Hitch (formulated in the 1970s by Alan Baddeley and Graham Hitch), which presents an alternative version of the short-term memory in which a central executive controls input from several slave systems such as the sensory memories.

Pick one of the four images on the next page. Spend three minutes observing the details, then close the book and draw the most accurate reproduction you can from memory using colored pencils. Now compare your drawing with the photo and spend another three minutes observing the same photo. Then close the book and draw the object a second time. Repeat this process as many times as you like and you should eventually create a detailed representation in your long-term memory.

Notice that this task doesn't just rely on your visual memory. For instance, if you have chosen the striped candies or the boots, you will almost certainly have consciously counted the five white stripes or the four white lace eyelets. Even people who are judged to have a photographic memory (eidetic memory, *see* page 53) often appear to "think" and make mental notes about what they view, rather than just blink their eyes and take a mental photograph. The autistic savant Stephen Wiltshire, who draws detailed pen and ink drawings of cityscapes from memory, admits, "When I am drawing I am thinking about the information and the details so I can memorize it and then draw it back."

TOPOGRAPHICAL
MEMORY

TOPOGRAPHICAL MEMORY INVOLVES THE ABILITY TO ORIENT OURSELVES IN SPACE, RECOGNIZE FAMILIAR PLACES, OR REMEMBER AND REPEAT A JOURNEY WE HAVE TAKEN.

It draws upon procedural memory because sometimes it involves a series of steps (turn right, walk forward three blocks, turn left at the church...) but it also requires the ability to imagine and recall places you have visited in no particular order (e.g. if you wanted to recall the three nearest gas stations to your home, you could mentally jump from one location to the other without making the whole journey).

In his book *The Brain's Sense of Movement,* Professor Alain Berthoz, an expert in the physiology of perception and action, says, "The ability to find one's way home or to memorize a route is not unique to humans; crabs return to the sea, bees to the hive, and desert ants to their nest using the sun to find their way. Each species has devised individual solutions to the same problem." The topographical memory feats of animals like the salmon (which battles hundreds of miles upstream heading home to breed) or the elephant (which develops a mental map of lifesaving water holes within vast areas of territory, passed down through successive generations) is also well known.

Scientists have spent decades attempting to understand the complex relationship between our vestibular apparatus (the non-auditory portion of the inner ear) and topographical memory. The vestibular system detects and tracks our movements, especially the neck, head, and eyes, and sends information about how fast we are moving to the brain, like a tachometer. The topographical memory tells us which route to follow, but our spatial orientation system also uses the vestibular information to work out the distance traveled.

All these systems work together to enable us to perform a complex operation such as walking from bed to bathroom in total darkness in the middle of the night. Alain Berthoz describes experiments that have led to "a fundamental concept: that vestibular memory is memory of movement, not of position... so the brain memorizes movement, not just places."

RABBIT MAZE

Here is a very simple demonstration of topographical memory in action. It would be impossible to complete this maze with your eyes closed, but thanks to your topographical memory, if someone else guided you to the carrot, you could find your way back to your starting position.

Close your eyes. Get a friend to place the book on the table in front of you (either sideways, upside-down, or the right way up) and then get them to place the index finger of your dominant hand on the page so that it's touching one of the rabbits. When you are ready, your friend must guide your finger firmly along the maze until it reaches the carrot that is farthest away. Make sure your fingertip stays in contact with the page during the journey. Now, keeping your eyes closed, move your finger across the page in a straight line and stop where you think your carrot hunt began. You should be able to do this with considerable accuracy, using your topographical memory.

DECLARATIVE MEMORY

DECLARATIVE MEMORY IS A FORM OF LONG-TERM MEMORY THAT IS ASSOCIATED WITH REMEMBERING FACTS AND KNOWLEDGE. IT CAN BE DIVIDED INTO TWO TYPES: EPISODIC MEMORY AND SEMANTIC MEMORY.

EPISODIC MEMORY

This is the memory of all the autobiographical events in your life: the places you have visited, the parties you have been to, the good and bad things that have happened to you, and all the other contextual data associated with these events, like the time and place, the emotions and physical feelings you experienced, who you were with, what you were wearing.

These memories are highly subjective and can also affect future behavior. For example, if you have a strong episodic memory of being stung by a bee when you were six years old and found it painful and frightening, you may develop a fear of bees and wasps in adult life and try to avoid them. Episodic memory is often represented by visual imagery, but sounds and smells can also be strong triggers for long-forgotten memories (or more accurately, memories we haven't consciously recalled for a long time). We can all be transported back to the places and emotions of childhood by a memorable smell—melting blacktop on a hot day, the sound of an ice cream truck, the antiseptic whiff of a hospital ward.

The recall of episodic memories often stirs up emotions because when an event occurs, emotion increases the likelihood that it will be recorded as a long-term memory. The fact that an event has been retained in your episodic memory in the first place is a strong indicator that it elicited powerful emotions while, or immediately after, it occurred.

HOW GOOD IS YOUR EPISODIC MEMORY?

There's little you can do to improve your episodic memory, but you can compensate by keeping a daily diary and rereading the previous day's entry each morning. As the following questions demonstrate, some episodic memories are easier to recall than others:

1. What did you have for breakfast this morning?

2. What did you have for breakfast yesterday?

3. What did you have for lunch the day before yesterday?

4. What did you have for breakfast on this day two years ago?

5. How did you celebrate your last birthday?

6. When and where was the last occasion that you injured yourself badly enough to require medical attention?

7. When was the last time you ate chocolate?

8. Why, when, and where was the last time you cried?

9. When and where was the last time and place that you drank a cup of coffee?

10. Can you remember an occasion as a child when you felt really proud?

SEMANTIC MEMORY

This is a more structured collection of facts, meanings, knowledge, and ideas, abstract and concrete, that you have learned that are part of the pool of human knowledge, independent of your own autobiographical relationship with this data. For example, your semantic memory of a table might include its appearance, associated vocabulary (e.g. trestle, dining room, furniture), function, construction materials, context (you'd expect to see one on the floor, but not up a tree). Much of semantic memory is abstract: if someone told you to draw a table, you could create a generic representation that most people in the world would recognize as a table because semantic knowledge is shared. You could also write the word "table" and communicate the same concept to anyone who shares the same semantic memory of this word.

We learn by experience so our semantic memories are often derived from our episodic memories. Past events in our lives can reinforce semantic memory, but gradually the episodic component becomes less important so eventually we can remember semantic information independently of when, where, and how we first learned it.

The answers to these five questions all require semantic memory. As you can see, we share a common pool of knowledge, but other semantic information is more specialized:

1. Name this object.

2. What color is it?

3. Pick two words that apply to this object:
   a) food
   b) furniture
   c) animal
   d) organic

4. Name the natural organic compound that gives this object its color.

5. True or false? This object contains the phytochemicals quercetin, phloridzin, and chlorogenic acid.

You can improve your semantic memory retention with the study skills on pages 117 to 139, but you can also improve your recall by using your intuition (which actually means paying attention to associated fragments that pop up from your semantic memory, with support from your episodic memory).

Ogi Ogas, a final-year Ph.D. student at Boston University's doctoral program in cognitive neuroscience, won $500,000 on the *Who Wants to be a Millionaire?* game show by using this technique: "The priming of a memory occurs because of the peculiar 'connectionist' neural dynamics of our cortex, where memories are distributed across many regions and neurons. If we can recall any fragment of a pattern, our brains tend to automatically fill in the rest."

The $250,000 question was "The department store Sears got its start by selling what specific product in its first catalog?" Ogi didn't know the answer immediately but the word "watches" came into his mind and he also felt intuitively that "railroads" were somehow relevant to the answer. He answered the question correctly and when he got home he researched online to discover that Richard Sears had been a railroad station agent in Redwood Falls, Minnesota, and sold gold pocket watches to other station agents along the line. He set up the R. W. Sears Watch Company and his first employee was watch repairman Alvah Curtis Roebuck, with whom he subsequently founded the mail-order catalog Sears, Roebuck & Company.

Here are ten general knowledge questions. If you don't know the answers, all the better; this will give you the opportunity to jump-start your semantic memory by accessing your episodic memory and brainstorming with associated semantic memory fragments to reach plausible answers.

While answering these questions, scribble down words and ideas associated with the topic as they occur to you. Don't disregard anything, however trivial. After you've looked up the answers on page 142, search Wikipedia for more information to see how some of your associated memory fragments could have led you to the answers.

1. Which sign of the zodiac is a person whose birthday is on October 18?

2. In which Asian country does the president live in The Blue House?

3. Whose parents were Andrew Bond and Monique Delacroix and how did they die?

4. Which is the largest joint in the body?

5. What was Elton John's birth name?

6. What is measured on the Beaufort scale?

7. Name the three flavors that make up a block of Neapolitan ice cream.

8. What does the "DC" stand for in DC Comics?

9. How is Mrs. O'Leary's cow said to have caused the great Chicago fire of 1871?

10. What type of nut is usually used to flavor macaroons?

PROCEDURAL MEMORY

This is a form of long-term memory of actions which, once acquired with practice, can subsequently be performed without any conscious process of recall (colloquially and rather misleadingly referred to as doing something "without thinking" or "with your eyes shut").

Procedural memory might include riding a bike, tying shoelaces, reading, juggling, driving a car—any skill that you once had to consciously learn but which you subsequently perform without the need for conscious control.

The acquisition phase of the skill requires practice, but this does not mean just repetition. Basic skill acquisition is achieved by making subtle changes and modifying behavior with each successive repetition, learning from feedback from previous performance to improve and refine present performance.

Literacy expert Dr. Dee Tadlock has developed the patented Read Right® program to support children who are struggling readers. Her procedural memory model uses a four-step predictive strategy along with a conscious awareness of the end result (rather than relying on a detailed understanding of a skill's components). The four steps are:

1) attempt;

2) fail;

3) analyze the result;

4) decide how to change the next attempt to achieve success.

You can use this method to acquire any skill. People who repeat the same task over and over again and fail to improve, miss out on the most important but also the most mentally and emotionally challenging steps—3 and 4. Albert Einstein famously said, "Insanity is doing the same thing over and over again and expecting different results," but he could equally have substituted the words "failure" or "mediocrity."

Repeating the same mistakes can build up bad habits and muscle memories of failure, which can be very difficult to unlearn later. Mindless repetition or rote learning can be an effective (though boring) strategy when approaching semantic memory tasks (see page 46), such as learning your multiplication tables or a list of French vocabulary, but it should be avoided at all costs when learning new skills and procedures, otherwise you will become an expert at repeating your mistakes.

In the early 1990s, Dr. K. Anders Ericsson, a psychology professor at Florida State University, introduced the idea that it takes 10,000 hours of practice to become world class at a particular skill (20 hours for 50 weeks a year for ten years, preferably by the age of 20). This figure was then popularized by Malcolm Gladwell as the "10,000-Hour Rule" in his best-selling book *Outliers*, which examines the factors that lead to high levels of success. However, as Geoff Colvin explains in his book, *Talent Is Overrated: What Really Separates World-Class Performers from Everybody Else,* the real issue is that irrespective of how many hours you put in, whether you want to improve or become world class, you have to engage in the right sort of "deliberate practice" (*see* page 69) which uses a model similar to Dr. Tadlock's.

CHOKING AND BEING CLUTCH

At times of extreme stress, experts who have spent years honing their skills can suddenly experience a form of analysis paralysis commonly known as "choking." Some of the most famous moments in sporting history have resulted from an individual or an entire team getting the chokes. One explanation for why this occurs is "explicit monitoring theory," which suggests that the performer suddenly becomes self-consciously aware of the step-by-step components of the skill, disrupting the procedural memory so that it momentarily ceases to be automatic.

The antithesis of choking is when expert performers are "in the zone," when procedural memory is uninhibited allowing optimal performance.

There is also a third variation which we call being "clutch": coming up with a big play when your team needs you, such as when an underdog rises to the occasion and beats a superior individual or team. The player with "clutch" achieves this by actually increasing his or her conscious awareness of the procedural performance. The same mechanism that causes an expert to choke can actually improve the performance of the relative novice.

EMOTION AND MEMORY

The most vivid events in episodic memory tend to be emotional. We recall events that have an emotional component with more clarity and detail than neutral events. For our Neolithic ancestors this would have been important for social bonding but it would also have been an important survival skill.

Individuals learned about the dangers of their environment through trial and error; there would have been a selective advantage for those who remembered emotional events, and an even greater advantage for those who remembered negative emotional events, as this could help them to avoid or escape similar dangers the next time they occurred. Modern humans retain this "negativity bias"—they have a greater recall of unpleasant memories compared with positive ones.

J. A. Easterbrook's Cue Utilization Theory (University of New Brunswick, Canada, 1959) proposes that when we experience an emotional event, high arousal leads to a narrowed focus-increased attention on the emotional component (the cues) and the causes of those emotions with a corresponding decrease in attention from other nonemotional parts of the stimulus. The emotional parts of the stimulus are encoded, while the other nonemotional details are neglected. This demonstrates once again that attention plays a key role in encoding, retention, and future recall.

This effect is responsible for a phenomenon called "weapon focus effect" in which witnesses to a violent crime can remember and describe the weapon in great detail, but have poor recall of the other details such as the attacker's clothing.

BULLET TIME

When people are placed in heightened emotional states, especially when they experience emergencies, such as a car crash, they frequently report the sensation of time slowing down. Scientists used to think that this was caused by the body producing epinephrine, making the brain think more quickly and providing a boost of energy to either run away from danger or fight. But recent experiments have shown this is not the case: it's a trick of memory.

Scientists at Baylor College of Medicine in Houston measured this apparent time-slowing effect by getting volunteers to jump backward and fall 48 feet into a safety net. During their descent the volunteers reached 70 mph (with no safety ropes), and even though it was completely safe, this terrifying experience produced the requisite fear.

As they fell, each subject was required to read out numbers that flashed onto a little video monitor that was strapped to their wrist. The rate at which the numbers flashed on and off the screen was calibrated so that it was a little too fast to be perceived under normal circumstances, but although subjects reported a perceived slowing of time, their ability to read the flashing numbers was not improved; their perception speeds did not increase.

SO WHAT REALLY HAPPENS IN YOUR BRAIN DURING AN EMERGENCY?

Deep in the brain's medial temporal lobe is an almond-shaped set of neurons called the amygdala which processes memory and emotional reactions. During times of heightened emotion, the amygdala becomes more active and encodes more memories per second than normal, and these memories are also stronger because of the emotional component.

The more memories you have of an event, the longer it appears to take. This also explains why childhood summers appear in retrospect to have been long and sunny: we lay down more memories as children because we are exposed to so many new stimuli and have a heightened emotional response to them; in adulthood we become more world-weary and less attentive to our surroundings.

On the next right-hand page there is a photo of an assailant holding a weapon. Turn the page, stare directly at the assailant and call firmly three times, "Police, drop your weapon!" Then close your eyes immediately, turn back to this page, open your eyes again and answer the questions below.

1.   Did you get a good look at the weapon? Write down a description of the gun: colors, shape, etc.
2.   Write down everything that you can remember about the assailant's physical appearance: clothes, jewelry, makeup, etc.
3.   How many ears did she have?

see explanation on page 142

EIDETIC MEMORY

COMMONLY REFERRED TO AS "PHOTOGRAPHIC MEMORY," EIDETIC MEMORY IS THE RARE ABILITY TO MEMORIZE SIGHTS, SOUNDS, AND OTHER OBJECTS WITH A VERY HIGH LEVEL OF DETAIL.

Visual and auditory memory are vitally important perceptual and learning skills. In sighted people, 80 percent of learning relies on the eyes while auditory memory is a key component of language acquisition and comprehension. Between two and ten percent of children appear to have visual eidetic abilities, but these diminish after the age of six as language and auditory memory become dominant.

Genuine eidetic ability in adulthood is very rare and is usually accompanied by significant cognitive deficits. The majority of true eidetic memorizers are developmentally delayed, as epitomized by the character Raymond Babbitt in the movie *Rain Man*. The real-life inspiration for this character was Kim Peek, an American savant, who was not autistic but was born without a corpus callosum, the band of white matter that connects the two hemispheres of the brain. Consequently, he could read quickly with high recall by scanning the left page with his left eye, and the right page with his right eye.

By contrast, most professional memorizers use techniques that they have spent many years practicing, although their memory feats appear so incomprehensible to the casual observer that they can easily be mistaken for eidetic memorizers.

The Russian composer and pianist Sergei Rachmaninov is said to have been able to perfectly recall any musical score after sight-reading it twice. He was unable to perform the same feat with a page of written text, however, so clearly it was a learned and specialized skill (albeit amazing), akin to that of the chess grandmasters who can recognize a huge number of viable chess positions, but fare no better than novice players when viewing a random configuration of pieces.

Mozart is probably the most well-known auditory eidetic. It is said that he could play a piece of music after listening to it only once, or conceive note-perfect symphonies in his head. However, Mozart was not born with the former skill and the latter is a myth, since his heavily annotated manuscripts show that he continually revised and reworked his compositions. Mozart's genius was largely the product of being intensively drilled from the age of three by a domineering father who was a famous composer and expert teacher.

Young Mozart was composing by the age of five, but many of his early compositions were heavily corrected by his father. Geoff Colvin points out in his book *Talent is Overrated* that "Wolfgang's first four piano concertos, composed when he was eleven, actually contain no original music by him. He put them together out of works by other composers." That is not to deny that he grew into one of the greatest composers who ever lived, but this was the result of "years of extremely hard, expert training."

AUTISTIC SAVANTS

Autistic savants who perform complex mental calculations have developed a highly specialized working memory, which allows them to "simply" perform a mental algorithm, unhindered by the distraction of normal social interaction. The right brain compensates for the left brain (*see* page 111), or maybe even has the luxury of being able to use all that left hemisphere brain space that isn't being gobbled up by language. Research has shown that savant abilities decrease as communication skills improve, so it seems that true eidetic ability can only be achieved by sacrificing areas of the brain that would normally be appropriated for resource-hungry socialization skills and other executive brain functions.

MUSICAL MEMORY

MUSICAL MEMORY IS THE ABILITY TO REMEMBER MUSIC-RELATED INFORMATION, INCLUDING NOTES, TONES, MUSICAL SEQUENCES (MELODIES, AND PITCHES. IT IS PRIMARILY NONVERBAL AND ENCODED DIFFERENTLY FROM LANGUAGE, ALTHOUGH IT IS PART OF AUDITORY MEMORY AND THE PHONOLOGICAL LOOP (WORKING MEMORY FOR MAINLY VERBAL INFORMATION).

Both the left and right sides of the brain are involved in processing music (in common with most brain tasks), but studies of patients with brain damage have led scientists to theorize that the left side of the brain is primarily responsible for long-term musical memory, while the right hemisphere is responsible for mediating access to this memory.

Memory expert Hervé Platel was one of the first scientists to explore the distinction between "musical semantic memory" and "verbal semantic memory," since "practically nothing is known about the functional anatomy of long-term memory for music."

He defines the former as "memory for 'well-known' melodies without any knowledge of the spatial or temporal circumstances of learning." He took PET scans of the brains of 11 subjects while they performed musical semantic memory and verbal semantic memory tasks, and discovered that different parts of the brain are activated for each kind of memory, although they share "a common network throughout the left-sided temporal neocortex."

Other research has looked at the relationship between musical and episodic memory. It has long been known that music can trigger memories, often emotional, but a recent study has shown where in the brain this occurs. Petr Janata, a cognitive neuroscientist at the University of California, Davis, scanned the brains of 13 volunteers while they were exposed to 30 different songs from the popular music chart, corresponding to the dates during which they were aged between 8 and 18. Subjects had to indicate when a piece of music triggered an autobiographical (episodic) memory.

Janata observed that the strongest episodic memories were accompanied by the most emotional responses, while the brain scans showed increased activity in the medial prefrontal cortex at these moments.

This study helps to explain why music can reach deep into the memories of patients with dementia. "What's striking is that the prefrontal cortex is among the last [of the brain regions] to atrophy," Janata notes. Patients who appear inert, depressed, and unresponsive can briefly reacquire their identities and become animated when played music from their earlier life. After the music stops, the positive effects continue: despite previously having been incapable of answering even the simplest questions, now briefly restored for a few minutes, they can talk, engage with others, and even sing.

HOW TO MEMORIZE A PIECE OF MUSIC

If you play an instrument you will know how elusive your musical memory can be. You think you know a piece inside out, then you take a music exam or perform on stage and suddenly your memory doesn't seem so solid. Worse still, performance anxiety threatens to make your mind go completely blank.

What can you do to commit a piece to memory, and then ensure that your memory doesn't choke when you have to play in public?

In later chapters we will discuss how people remember objects in a spatial relationship (*see* page 85) and use landmarks to remember objects outdoors (*see* page 87).

Well, the same happens with playing an instrument. If you have learned to perform a piece in one location, your memories become associated with and, to a certain extent, dependent on that place. You can tune out your surroundings because they are familiar, but when you move to another location, with different sight lines and a different acoustic environment, your music memory has to compete with all these added stimuli and the task becomes much harder.

So, if possible, before a performance or exam, try to replicate those conditions, so your brain doesn't have to take up processing space to block out new stimuli.

FOLLOW THESE TIPS WHEN PRACTICING

1. Analyze the structure of the piece. Not only will this improve your interpretation of the music but it will provide a mental scaffold on which to build your musical memory. Suzuki piano teacher Jenny Macmillan says, "Researchers agree that it is essential to support memory of the sounds, movements, and sight with analysis of the forms and harmonies of the music. In this way, material to be remembered is related to other relevant information."

2. Listen to other performances so that long before you can play the piece yourself, you can hum or sing it, or hear the music in your head.

3. Break the piece down into small phrases and practice those. (Use slow-motion practice to improve your retention as well as intonation—*see* page 75).

4. Start memorizing early in the learning process so that you memorize sections, as this will help improve your ability to interpret the music.

5. When you make a mistake, try to fix it from memory, rather than looking at the score. This helps to reinforce retrieval pathways in the brain. Only then, check the score to make sure you're correct.

6. Don't always start at the beginning, because you will end up familiar with the beginning and less familiar with the end. Start in different places, so you don't become over-reliant on continuity and momentum to play the piece.

7. Practice frequently and in different locations, for the reasons already discussed.

8. Rehearse in your mind. Performance psychologist Dr. Noa Kageyama says, "In one study, participants who mentally practiced a five-finger sequence on an imaginary piano for two hours a day had the same neurological changes (and reduction in mistakes) as the participants who physically practiced the same passage on an actual piano." Mental rehearsal activates the same neural pathways as physical practice.

9. Concentrate on the beauty and musicality of the piece rather than the technical details. Make interpretation and expressive musicality your goal, so that any technical attention is a means to this end, rather than a sterile, mechanistic end in itself. Canadian child prodigy Jan Lisiecki was performing in concert halls around the world by the time he was 14. According to violinist and conductor Pinchas Zukerman, "talent of that magnitude comes at least two or three generations apart." Jan says, "I just want to always express how beautiful the music is, how beautifully the composer wrote the music, and not how beautifully I can play it or how fast I can play it, I mean, it's all interpretation but I feel that the interpretation is actually to make the music more beautiful."

HYPERTHYMESIA

A relative of eidetic memory is an extremely rare phenomenon called hyperthymesia, a highly superior episodic memory. Fewer than 30 documented cases of hyperthymesia have been confirmed in peer-reviewed articles. The first reported case was Jill Rosenberg (known in case literature as AJ) in 2006, who can recall details from every day of her life from when she was 14 years old, including events that she read or watched in the media: "Starting on February 5, 1980, I remember everything. That was a Tuesday." She has also suffered from depression because among all the memories which spring unbidden into her consciousness, she is plagued by bad ones: "It's like an endless, chaotic film that can completely overpower me. And there's no stop button."

She has also kept a diary obsessively since she was ten and she compulsively hoards objects and personal memorabilia, which help her to organize and make sense of all the information. It is unclear whether her obsessive traits are causal or consequential or a mixture of both, but she doesn't have to make a special effort to remember the events of her life; instead she lacks the ability to forget them.

DO YOU HAVE A PHOTOGRAPHIC MEMORY?

Probably not, but take this test and see. Focus on the white dot on the first image for ten seconds, then quickly shift your focus to the white dot on the second image.

Everyone keeps a residual image of the first photo for a fraction of a second, enabling them to glimpse the full color image for a fleeting moment when they look at the second photo. However, if you have an eidetic visual memory, you will see a full color image for much longer, maybe even several seconds.

RECOGNITION VS. RECALL

WHICH TESTS DO YOU PREFER: MULTIPLE CHOICE OR THOSE WHERE YOU HAVE TO THINK UP THE ANSWERS ALL BY YOURSELF?

Most people prefer the former because the skill required for multiple choice questions is *recognition,* which is generally easier than *recall,* unless you lose confidence and get led astray by the wrong answers.

When pricing products, supermarkets are very conscious of the distinction between recognition and recall. The price of an item is clearly a salient factor in whether a shopper makes a purchase. Consumer research shows that people have a price range for how much they are prepared to pay. If an item is near the bottom of this price range, it is considered good value and if it is near the top it is considered expensive, which is where other factors come into play such as branding, quality, freshness, etc. When asked to name the price of a particular item, however, many people have difficulty remembering what they paid the last time, although they can recognize whether the price has gone up or down.

Shoppers who remember specific prices and use them to guide purchasing decisions are classified as "price aware"; shoppers who cannot remember specific prices and base their decisions on price differentials are classified as "price conscious." Your memory has a significant impact on your shopping experience and purchasing behavior, and store promotions target "price aware" and "price conscious" shoppers using different strategies.

Here are five items and their prices. Study them for ten seconds and then turn the page.

| 50¢ | $1.15 | 65¢ | $1.00 | $2.00 |

YOUR LOCAL SUPERMARKET HAS A BOGO PROMOTION ON RED APPLES

A single red apple costs $1 but the "buy one, get one free" offer means you can pick up two apples for 50 cents each.

1. Can you remember the original price of a red apple on the previous page?

2. If not, do you have a rough idea what the price was (write down a range)?

3. What percentage of the second red apple is "free"?

Now read on to discover whether you snapped up a bargain.

BOGO

The ever-popular BOGO (buy one, get one free) targets both the price-aware and the price-conscious consumer, by exploiting not only sloppy math skills but also their poor memories.

The bigger the price differential, the higher the margin on a familiar and simple offer like this one. Most people are aware that the BOGO usually involves raising the nominal price of the first item so that the second item is not completely free. In fact it isn't even close to free and in many cases it isn't even half price.

You paid $1 for a red apple in the BOGO promotion. Ordinarily the price of the apple was 65¢, but with the BOGO, each apple cost you 50¢, a saving of 15¢ per apple at the old price.

Still think you know how much of the second apple was free?

At these new prices the second apple isn't free; it isn't even half price. You have paid an extra 35¢ (about 54 percent) so only 46 percent of the second apple is free. Or put another way, that's about this much: →

62

WHAT KIND OF LEARNER ARE YOU?

ALTHOUGH IT IS POSSIBLE TO LEARN THROUGH A COMBINATION OF STYLES, LEARNERS ARE PREDOMINANTLY EITHER VISUAL, AUDITORY, OR KINESTHETIC.

This quiz will test which one applies to you. Once you know your learning strengths and weaknesses you can ensure that you choose learning strategies that play to your strengths.

Read all 60 questions and make a note every time you answer "yes" to a question. Only answer "yes" if you strongly identify with the statement and feel that it applies to you. If you are ambivalent or disagree with the statement, move on to the next question. Make a note of how many yes answers you give for each section. If one section stands out for you with a lot of yes answers, then that is your predominant learning style. If your answers are evenly spread between two or more sections, then you are a mixture (e.g. auditory-visual).

VISUAL

1. I have neat, legible handwriting.
2. I am really good at spelling; I also believe that good spelling is very important.
3. I prefer video conferencing to a telephone conversation. I like to be able to see the face of the other person so I can better judge what they are saying and feeling.
4. I remember faces but forget names.
5. I find PowerPoint presentations and diagrams very useful.
6. I like to sit at the front of the classroom so I don't get distracted by others.
7. I learn best on my own from books, rather than in a group.
8. When someone asks me to buy a few things from the supermarket, I prefer to write a list than keep them in my head.

9. When faced with a challenging unfamiliar task, I will look online for information or read a book to teach myself. I usually read instructions before attempting any task.

10. I often write things down and take detailed notes.

11. I spend time preparing and reading up on a subject rather than following my gut instinct or jumping right in.

12. If I had to learn lines for a play, I would study the script and practice the thoughts and words in my head, rather than out loud.

13. I get easily distracted by background noise and have difficulty concentrating when several people are talking.

14. I notice the visual similarities and differences between things that other people miss.

15. I'm a fast reader.

16. When I do a crossword, I like to see the clue and see the squares and letters for myself rather than listen to someone else read them out.

17. I am very good at imagining scenes in my head.

18. Unless someone expresses emotion with their face, I tend to overlook how they might really be feeling.

19. I learn well when someone demonstrates a physical task or solves a problem by performing the activity themselves while I watch (and maybe take notes).

20. I don't like listening to too much explanation or verbal lecturing; I could learn the same information more quickly on my own by reading a book.

AUDITORY

1. I understand and remember things better when I or someone else says them out loud.

2. I enjoy learning foreign languages and find them quite easy.

3. I can easily articulate my ideas because I'm a good talker.

4. When I meet someone for the second time, I usually have no trouble remembering their name.

5. While someone is explaining something to me, I might look away from them or close my eyes so I can concentrate better.

6. I prefer telephone conversations to video conferencing. I find the visual information distracting.

7. I pick up subtle clues by listening to other people's choice of words and tone of voice rather than the expression on their face.

8. I often talk to myself while I work.

9. Faced with an unfamiliar task, I'm happy to ask someone to explain it to me.

10. I'm not a fast reader. Sometimes I move my lips while I read.

11. I'm good at remembering spoken lists, such as when it's my turn to buy a round at the bar.

12. I'm a good listener.

13. I can understand verbal instructions easily and rarely have to ask for a question to be repeated.

14. I talk to myself to verbalize things I want to remember.

15. I'm good at telling stories and jokes.

16. I learn best by talking and bouncing my ideas off other people and I enjoy studying with a partner or in a group because I can ask questions, discuss, and hear information and ideas.

17. If I had to learn lines for a play, I would record myself saying them and then listen to the recording.

18. I'm quite articulate and not afraid to talk out loud in class.

19. I would prefer to give an oral presentation than produce a written report.

20. I'm very musical.

KINESTHETIC

1. People say I have illegible handwriting and my spelling's none too impressive either.

2. I will often jump right into doing something without asking how to do it, because there's no better way to learn than by just getting into it.

3. I enjoy playing sports.

4. I can do a lot of things, but they can be difficult to explain in words.

5. When I meet someone for the second time, I might have trouble remembering their name but I have a clear memory of what happened the last time we were together.

6. I enjoy doing practical puzzles that I can solve with my hands.

7. I tend to doodle while I'm on the phone.

8. I find taking long tests or writing essays boring. I often become restless and want to do something physical instead.

9. Faced with a challenging task, I just kind of figure it out as I go along by trying things out. I'll usually only read the instructions as a last resort.

10. My favorite kind of films are action movies. My worst kind of film involves people sitting around a table talking to each other and nothing's happening.

11. I like "getting my hands dirty" and need to be physically active.

12. I tend to follow my gut instinct.

13. If something was bothering me, I'd be more likely to go for a run or go to the gym than sit at home thinking it through.

14. I get really bored and confused when someone tries to explain something by giving me lots of instructions.

15. I don't like sitting down for too long. It makes me feel jittery.

16. I love making and building things or taking them apart.

17. I prefer to try something out, rather than have someone else show me.

18. I use my hands a lot and move my body when I am explaining something, or I might draw a diagram instead.

19. Other people say I'm hyperactive.

20. I understand things best when I can touch or do them.

Here are ten ways to maximize your learning by targeting your learning style. If you are a mixture of styles, use the suggestions from two or more relevant sections.

VISUAL LEARNERS

You learn best by seeing, and it is easiest for you to remember the things you've seen, so adapt your studying to suit your visual learning style:

1. Find a quiet place to study alone, and make your study area visually appealing.

2. Write down lots of notes and make lists to help you organize your thoughts and ideas.

3. Reread your notes immediately after a class because seeing the written words will reinforce your memory retention more than with other types of learners.

4. Use maps, charts, diagrams, mind maps, and outlines—anything that represents information visually. Just writing something down and making an outline will help you to learn.

5. Watch videos and documentaries about the subject you are studying.

6. Highlight keywords and ideas using different highlighter pens to structure information visually.

7. Use flashcards.

8. You need time to think the materials through before understanding, so allow yourself this reading and thinking time to help you process the information.

9. Sit at the front of the class so that you can clearly see the teacher's facial expressions and body language because you are sensitive to visual cues.

10. When you hear a new word, write it down so that you have a strong visual representation of the sound, then look it up in the dictionary.

AUDITORY LEARNERS

You learn best by listening, and it is easiest for you to remember the things you've heard, so adapt your studying to suit your auditory learning style:

1. Study with a friend or study group so that you can talk out loud and hear the information. The more times you can hear the information, the easier it will be to understand and encode in your strong auditory memory.

2. Record lectures so that you can sit and listen without taking notes; listen back to them later and then make notes.

3. Recite information out loud that you want to understand or remember, even when you are studying alone.

4. When solving a problem, talk through various options to yourself.

5. Listen to audio tapes and documentaries about the subject you are studying.

6. Sit to the side or near the back of the class so you can concentrate on listening rather than staring at the teacher's face and trying to look attentive.

7. Use rhymes and mnemonics to help you remember lists and recite them out loud.

8. Reinforce your comprehension and memory by explaining concepts to your study partner and getting them to verbally quiz you.

9. If you are having trouble recalling information, close your eyes to block out visual distractions and try to hear the answer. Talk to yourself to prime your memory by association.

10. When writing a first draft, type or write the words and thoughts that you hear in your head without worrying about spelling and grammar; just get the words down on paper and then go back and fix the other details.

KINESTHETIC LEARNERS

You learn best by touching and manipulating objects and involving your body, and it is easiest for you to remember the things you've experienced physically, so adapt your studying to suit your kinesthetic learning style:

1. Take a walk or pace around the room while you read aloud from a book or notecards, or go for a run while listening to the information on an MP3 player.

2. Involve your body in the learning task. If you are reading information on a screen, mouse-click on the words to give a physical feedback to your reading.

3. Knead a stress ball in your hand, chew gum, or doodle ideas and thoughts while you are learning.

4. Use flashcards, because you can touch them, move them, shuffle them, and interact with them physically.

5. If you can't experience something physically, try to imagine yourself physically climbing into a problem to grasp what makes it work.

6. Study in short blocks of time and when you start to get jittery, take a quick break and do something physical, like walking outside for a few minutes.

7. Try to make everything you learn as concrete as possible and relate the information to your everyday life. For example, if you were working on Pythagoras's theorem, build a right-angled triangle with some wooden sticks or straws and manipulate this object with your hands in real time and space to deepen your understanding.

8. Where possible, type rather than write, because it gives more concrete and immediate feedback for the kinesthetic learner and keeps you physically engaged in the process.

9. Vary your activities and don't force yourself to spend too long on one task. You study just as hard as visual and auditory learners, but you benefit from mixing things up a bit more than they do.

10. Wherever possible, use physical objects to support your learning.

TALENT IS OVERRATED, DELIBERATE PRACTICE
BRINGS SUCCESS

In 2007, psychologists K. Anders Ericsson, Michael J. Prietula, and Edward T. Cokely published the article "The Making of an Expert" in the *Harvard Business Review*, making a provocative and challenging assertion for anyone seeking greatness. They declared: "New research shows that outstanding performance is the product of years of deliberate practice and coaching, not of any innate talent or skill."

The article cites the case of two Hungarian educators, László and Klara Polgár, who 40 years ago deliberately set out to show that geniuses are made, not born, and to challenge the popular assumption that women couldn't excel at chess, then a predominantly male-dominated activity. They systematically trained their three daughters intensively in chess from an early age; all three went on to gain top ten ranking in the world among female chess players. Judit, the youngest, achieved the title of grand master at the age of 15 years and 4 months, the youngest person of either gender to do so until then. She has since defeated ten current or former world champions.

So what exactly is "deliberate practice" and what else do you need to engage in it?

1. You must invest time. Ericsson says, "Our research shows that even the most gifted performers need a minimum of ten years (or 10,000 hours) of intense training before they win international competitions."

2. Geoff Colvin gives a comprehensive description of deliberate practice in his book, *Talent is Overrated: What Really Separates World-Class Performers from Everybody Else*: "It is activity designed specifically to improve performance... it can be repeated a lot; feedback on results is continuously available; it is highly demanding mentally ... and it isn't much fun."

3. Practicing must be supervised by an expert teacher, who is "capable of giving constructive, even painful, feedback" and can help devise strategies for improvement.

4. The student must be highly motivated and actively seek out this feedback.

5. When the student's future development eventually exceeds the teacher's level of expertise, the student must find a more expert teacher.

NINE SECRETS OF DELIBERATE PRACTICE

1. Find an expert coach. You need constant feedback from experts whom you trust and respect, otherwise you cannot recognize your mistakes or devise a strategy for improvement.

2. Don't practice the things you are already good at. It may be more fun and less work, but if you want to turn a hobby into real expertise, you must concentrate most of your effort on developing your weak points.

3. To work on your weaknesses you must first admit to yourself that you are worse than you want to be and then you have to believe you CAN and WILL improve—otherwise you will lack motivation during the mentally and/or physically demanding process of deliberate practice.

4. You have to love something to excel at it but this doesn't mean that you will enjoy yourself all the time. If you want to love doing something all the time, just treat it as a hobby but don't complain when you don't improve.

5. A study of London taxi drivers—who train for two years to memorize the routes through the city streets to acquire "The Knowledge"—showed brain growth in the area of the brain which processes spatial awareness. Accept that your brain and episodic memory is like a muscle and needs training to develop.

6. Without daily physical training, no amount of positive thinking, vision, "clutch" (see page 50), or desire to be the best will enable a regular person to sprint 330 feet in under ten seconds. In a very real way, the same applies to the brain's cognitive control and executive functions.

7. Living in a cave does not make you a geologist.

8. Deliberate practice requires—but is also a key component of—self-regulation. Before practice you should set clear goals for the session that also focus on the process of reaching that goal. During the session, you focus on the important self-regulatory skill of self-observation: "For example, ordinary endurance runners in a race tend to think about anything other than what they're doing; it's painful... Elite runners, by contrast, focus intensely on themselves." After the practice session comes the all-important self-regulatory feedback and evaluation. Without this continual metacognition, the practice is incomplete.

9. Live by Thomas Edison's famous observation that "vision without execution is hallucination" and Sam Mendes's 25th Rule for Directors: "Never, ever, ever forget how lucky you are to do something that you love."

LIVELY REPETITION VS.
ROTE LEARNING

THERE'S A LONG-RUNNING DEBATE ABOUT THE ROLE OF REPETITION IN LEARNING. CERTAIN TYPES OF REPETITION SUCH AS "ROTE" LEARNING ARE OFTEN HAILED BY EDUCATIONAL TRADITIONALISTS AS THE WAY TO RAISE FALLING STANDARDS AND GET BACK TO BASICS; PROGRESSIVE EDUCATORS VIEW THEM AS THE ANTITHESIS OF CREATIVE AND ENGAGING EDUCATION. BUT WHO IS RIGHT?

The answer is they are both right (and both wrong). There's nothing wrong with lively repetition (LR) so long as you don't base an entire educational system on it. Don't be afraid to use it; you won't turn your brain to jelly.

It also depends on the context in which rote learning is used and how "fun" you think learning and memorizing should be. Rote learning can be an effective way to memorize certain types of information and activate specific types of memory but it is very damaging when applied to the wrong kind of memory task.

Opponents of rote learning instinctively believe that the only effective learning is fun learning, and that the carrot is always better than the stick. Opponents of learning "parrot fashion" argue that it's boring and paternalistic and that it stifles critical thinking. However, as the previous section has demonstrated, learning and development aren't always fun. In fact, self-development can be highly demanding and downright unpleasant (ask any Olympic champion). Besides, numerous studies into learning and motivation have shown that people aren't always motivated by what we think they are.

In 1968, American psychologist and business management guru, Frederick Herzberg, published a famous article, "One More Time: How Do You Motivate Employees?" in the *Harvard Business Review,* in which he challenged nine myths about motivation. He argued that shorter working hours, spiraling wages, and fringe benefits did not increase motivation in the long run. That sounds like a gift to thrifty or unscrupulous employers.

So what does motivate them? Don't be unduly influenced by Dr. Herzberg's PhD in electric shock therapy.)

In fact, it turns out that the main motivators are, in descending order of importance: a sense of achievement, recognition, the work itself, increasing responsibility, and opportunity for advancement and growth.

So where does rote learning fit into all this? The main issue appears to be compliance. Rote learning is most effective when the learner is engaged and motivated to perform, rather than have it imposed from above. As modern motivational expert Daniel H. Pink says in his best-seller, *Drive: The Surprising Truth About What Motivates Us,* "Living a satisfying life requires more than simply meeting the demands of those in control. Yet in our offices and our classrooms we have way too much compliance and way too little engagement."

So when an educator sets up a rote learning group session, he or she should give the students a sense of ownership and devise ways of demonstrating to them that the rote memory task is not an exercise in mute submission, but a useful memory tool when used for the appropriate memory tasks. Maybe it's time to rebrand rote learning and rename it "lively repetition."

LEARNING SOMETHING BY LIVELY REPETITION

In her book, *Battle Hymn of the Tiger Mother,* Amy Chua insists: "Tenacious practice, practice, practice is crucial for excellence; rote repetition is underrated in America."

First, let's be clear that lively repetition (LR) is not the same as the "deliberate practice" of the previous chapter. It should never be used for episodic memory tasks (learning a skill) or for tasks which require critical thinking. These demand entirely different tools.

Furthermore, it is important to stress once again that the motivation for LR should be intrinsic, not, as Amy Chua argues, extrinsic which, as many educators and psychologists agree, comes at too great an emotional and intellectual cost. It can be a great way to get people to do boring tasks, but it stifles creative thinking and, in the long run, reduces self-esteem.

WHEN YOU WANT TO LEARN SOMETHING BY LR

1. LR should only be used for quick, routine memorizing of lists of information, such as the periodic table, multiplication tables, mathematical formulas, anatomy in medicine, etc.

2. Don't be boring. Lively repetition should be fun and feel good. Don't dismiss a useful tool just because it's become synonymous with the teaching styles of authoritarian regimes and sharp-elbowed parents.

3. Learning something by heart can provide the most important motivator on Herzberg's list: a sense of achievement. When you've memorized something completely you'll feel an endorphin-releasing sense of accomplishment.

4. Use chunking (*see* page 79) and rhythm to break the text into memorable packets of auditory information. The brain thrives on rhythm and repetition for these kinds of tasks, because the longer the information can be kept in your short-term memory, the more effectively it can be transferred to your long-term memory.

5. Search for a song and if you can't find one, make one up. There are five-year-olds who can name all fifty U.S. states—the YouTube channel "Acroanna" features one of them—a smiling five-year-old named Annie singing a mnemonic song. For a more geographical approach, other songs teach the states going up and down the country from west to east.

6. Recite or sing out loud. There's a good reason for this: it rehearses the information in your auditory short-term memory, and ... *the longer the information can be kept in your short-term memory, the more effectively it can be transferred to your long-term memory.*

7. Use your body (especially if you're a kinesthetic learner—*see* page 65). Devise a dance or hand-clapping sequence, anything that makes you move your body as you sing or recite your text.

8. Complete this sentence without looking back:

THE LONGER THE INFORMATION CAN BE KEPT IN YOUR

. . . .

THE MORE EFFECTIVELY IT CAN BE TRANSFERRED TO YOUR

. . . .

MUSCLE MEMORY AND
MINDFUL PRACTICE

Muscle memory is the ability for muscles to remember a sequence of movements; it is part of your procedural memory (*see* page 49) but it also takes place in your muscles (it's not all in the brain). When you catch a ball or even open a door, you depend on muscle memory.

Apart from repetition, two other techniques that sportspeople, martial artists, and dancers use to boost muscle memory of a physical routine are slow motion and exaggeration, which come together under the umbrella of "mindful practice." This is distinct from deliberate practice (*see* page 69) because it is process-oriented rather than goal-oriented. Despite appearances, slow, mindful movement is a powerful and dynamic way to teach mind and body to learn new skills and to develop coordination. Repetition is an important component—routines must be practiced over and over again—but attention, awareness, and ease of movement are paramount.

MARTIAL ARTS

Martial artists use slow, gentle, and sometimes exaggerated movements to learn and practice correct form and technique. Many people struggle to understand how slow motion blocking, punching, and kicking can be applicable to a real fight. Danny Larusso, the bullied teen in the movie *The Karate Kid,* shares these misgivings. His sensei, Mr Miyagi, makes him clean and polish cars and paint fences day after day, with the iconic instruction "Wax on, wax off." Only later does Danny realize that these slow and exaggerated movements have trained his muscle memory for high-speed combat.

MOUNTAIN BIKING

Mountain bikers use an important technique called pumping to increase speed by directing forward, upward, and downward momentum, gain traction, and control the height on jumps. Professional mountain biker, BMX rider, and coach Tom Dowie explains how he teaches his students to learn the crucial pumping technique: "I always say it's better to overexaggerate the movement at first to find the feeling yourself and to train your body to the muscle memory of the movement. Try and feel the movement more than think it as you're applying it, it's trusting your brain's already processed it and letting your body go with it."

GOLF

The pioneering American professional golfer Ben Hogan practically invented practice golf and famously spent years researching and experimenting with different methods of swing. Slow motion practice was crucial to making his swing one of the greatest in the history of the game. Slow motion allowed him to recognize his weaknesses and correct them, often in the middle of a tournament. Sometimes he would get up in the night to practice in slow motion in a mirror, to pinpoint the issues that had hindered him during that day's play, so that he could be match-ready the following morning.

WOODSHEDDING

Many music teachers advocate slow practice to develop physical skill and concentration. Playing a piece slowly allows musicians to focus with greater detail on the notes, fingering, intonation, articulation, tone, rhythm, and dynamics, and to notice how small changes can affect the outcome. Violinist and Philadelphia Orchestra concertmaster David Kim explains how he uses mindful super-slow woodshedding (a musician's term meaning private practice): "When you're trying to teach a young person a new language, you repeat a certain word seven times... when I find a difficult spot ... I'll literally kind of woodshed really slowly, I try to do note by note... I'll do the shifts back and forth, minimum seven times, even if they are going well." This detailed slow motion work gives him a powerful feeling of solidity and assurance when he is performing on stage.

THE FELDENKRAIS METHOD

The Feldenkrais Method, used by actors, dancers, and therapists, is a dynamic system that increases self-awareness by breaking movements down into their smallest parts and looking at them in relation to gravity. Its originator, Israeli physicist Moshé Feldenkrais, "devised a series of quiet, exploratory exercises that allow the brain to learn new skills, to evoke new neuromuscular patterns of organic movement and thought. The exercises are slow, gentle, and controlled." This deepens the awareness of how you use your body and increases efficiency. It teaches the brain to create effective movement; it teaches the body to serve the brain's intentions. In fact, a key question in Feldenkrais is "What will best serve my intentions?"

Slow, mindful movement increases attention and awareness, which are major preconditions for brain neuroplasticity to occur. Movements should not be repeated by rote; they organically serve intention. Michael Merzenich, a leading neuroscientist in the field of brain neuroplasticity and a supporter of Feldenkrais, stresses, "One of the lessons of this research is that stereotypy is the enemy. And that you really want to exercise the brain with a variety of movements, a variety of actions. A variety of challenges."

TAKE AN EXTENDED COFFEE BREAK

Try this with a cup of coffee. Take *four minutes* to reach for a drink, bring the cup to your lips, take a sip, and return the cup to the table. It's fascinating and you will learn surprising details about the quality and efficiency of your body movements.

It's actually quite hard to do. At first, most people go too fast. You need to allow about 45 seconds to reach for the cup, another 45 seconds to bring the cup to your lips, 45 seconds to drink, 45 seconds to return the cup to the table, and 45 seconds to return to your starting position. That still leaves another 15 seconds to fill. So slow down even more!

You've been using a cup without dribbling or scalding yourself for years now, so you probably think there's nothing more to learn. Yet, if you slow the whole process down you will be viewing something you take for granted with new eyes; not only will it make you realize what amazing coordination is required for the simplest of tasks, but you will notice areas where you could make the movement more efficient. For instance, you might find that you grip the handle too tightly or that you hold tension in your jaw. You might discover that you stick your tongue out or crane your neck forward unnecessarily in anticipation of the cup reaching your lips.

WEBER'S LAW

One of the psychophysical mechanisms that supports slow motion and mindful practice is Weber's law, which states that "The change in a stimulus that will be just noticeable is a constant ratio of the original stimulus."

Imagine you were carrying a pile of five books and someone placed another book on top of the pile—you would notice it. But if you were carrying a huge box containing a hundred books, you wouldn't notice the weight of one extra book.

The same principle applies to movement. Slowing down a movement and extending its range (exaggeration) allows you to notice more subtle variations in that movement, making it easier for you to apply the correct form and technique, achieve maximum efficiency, and nail every single little detail.

MUSCLE MEMORY ISN'T JUST IN THE BRAIN

Brain neuroplasticity and the developing of skills shows up as increased brain mass in specific memory areas; the same is true of muscle memory, which results in physical and chemical changes in the muscle. It's well known in sports science that athletes can quickly regain lost muscle mass, strength, flexibility, and coordination when they return to training after a long period of inactivity, because strength training permanently increases the number of cell nuclei within the muscle fibers. This is why sports, especially strength training, at an early age can have lasting benefits in adulthood.

TEN TIPS FOR SLOW MOTION PRACTICE

Slow motion practice can improve any skill that involves physical movement, whether it's your golf swing or getting out of a chair efficiently without putting too much stress on your back, neck, and knees.

1. Focus on the present moment; concentrate on the process rather than a goal.

2. Be aware of your breathing. Breathe in through your nose and out through your mouth. Don't hold your breath. Observe how you combine the breath with the movement. Slow motion movement will reveal any areas where they are in conflict.

3. Imagine joints and bones moving, rather than muscles contracting, relaxing, and doing work.

4. Try to make the movements effortless. This will help the movement to flow but it will also highlight the places where you are using too much effort.

5. Break down big tasks into smaller and smaller ones so that you can examine and perform the tiniest possible components.

6. When you identify an area of weakness, try to perform the action well at least seven times before moving on to the next component.

7. Complete the whole movement. Slow motion allows you to see where you are cutting movement short and not using the full range of your body's capabilities, or curtailing a physical action.

8. Make slow, mindful practice a habit because you will gain maximum benefit if you use it regularly in a structured and consistent way.

9. If it is safe to do so, perform the slow motion activity at least once with your eyes shut.

10. Slow motion practice doesn't have to be real; you can visualize. Mental imagery has a huge impact on sports, and professional sportspeople now habitually use slow motion visualization to focus on technique.

CHUNKING
AND PATTERNS

MOST OF US CAN RELIABLY STORE BETWEEN FOUR AND SEVEN ITEMS IN OUR WORKING MEMORY. IF YOU THINK THAT'S POOR, YOU'D BE RIGHT, AT LEAST COMPARED TO AN ANIMAL WITH WHICH WE SHARE 98.8 PERCENT OF OUR DNA—THE CHIMPANZEE.

At the Primate Research Institute of Kyoto University, Professor Tetsuro Matsuzawa has spent years conducting cognitive tests on Ai, a 36-year-old chimpanzee, and her 13-year-old son, Ayumu, to discover that chimps have extraordinary memories. Matsuzawa says, "They can grasp things at a glance. As a human, you can do things to improve your memory, but you will never be a match for Ayumu." The chimpanzees can locate in sequence the numerals 1 to 9 spread randomly across a computer screen and then covered by white squares, after originally seeing them for only a fraction of a second.

However, something special separates us from chimps, remarkable though they are. Our delight in pattern recognition allows us to boost our working memory by consciously splitting up information into more memorable chunks. Furthermore, according to neuroscientist Daniel Bor, a research fellow at the University of Sussex in England and author of *The Ravenous Brain: How the New Science of Consciousness Explains Our Insatiable Search for Meaning*, the human desire to find patterns is the very source of human creativity.

Find patterns and use chunking when you need to remember a group of numbers or letters or even a group of objects. You do this already with telephone numbers and when reciting the alphabet. Try to link the material to something in your previous experience that forms a memorable pattern. When someone gives you a twelve-digit number to memorize, use chunking to split it into three groups of four. The number 159407201969 is much easier to remember as 1594 0720 1969 and even easier still if you spot that 0720 1969 (July 20, 1969) was the date that Neil Armstrong stepped onto the surface of the moon.

CAN YOU SPOT THE RELATIONSHIP BETWEEN THE SYMBOLS AND THE NUMBERS?

USE CHUNKING TO CRACK THE CODE:

267	3	5	*GREEN*
5	67	48	*RED*
49	9	2	*ORANGE*
–	– –	–	*BLUE*
	– –	– – –	*WHITE*
– –	–	–	*YELLOW*

HOW CAN THIS MYTHICAL BEAST HELP YOU REMEMBER THESE SIX ANIMALS?

SEQUENCES

HERE IS A DELICIOUS BOX OF 24 CHOCOLATES, WHICH YOU ARE GOING TO LEARN, IN THE CORRECT ORDER, WITHIN THE NEXT SEVEN MINUTES.

On page 84 an empty tray needs filling. Take a quick look. Scary isn't it? Twenty-four little cubicles that you are going to fill up in the correct order without making any errors.

First, let's try your customary method. Give yourself a minute to stare blankly at the top two rows while your anxiety levels slowly rise! Then turn the page and see how you get on.

WELL, HERE'S THE EMPTY TRAY. YOU HAVE TWO MINUTES TO FILL IT UP.

Now, one of two things will have happened. Either you will have remembered the positions of a few standout pralines (like the blue shiny one, or the striped one) and then tried to fit the others around them, or you will have become so confused by the new configuration that it will have interfered with your fragile memory, leaving you totally confused.

However, don't despair. The reason you struggled is that these abstract symbols don't hold any meaning for you, apart from looking good enough to eat. If they were letters or numbers, you'd be able to say them out loud, using chunking (*see* page 79) to keep them in your auditory memory long enough to fill the blank boxes. But how do you remember 24 fairly similar abstract items? In four minutes. Yes, four (you've used three already). So what's the solution? Create a story.

This is just one example and it won't be entirely suitable for you because it hasn't come from your head and it isn't your personal set of visual associations, so you may want to write your own. (Incidentally, when you've mastered this technique, you'll be able to reduce seven minutes to two.)

The story is inspired by shapes and other visual details. Read the story three times (if you're an auditory learner, read it aloud each time) and then turn the page. Now use the story to recall the correct order of the chocolates and you should be able to remember many more chocolates than you did before.

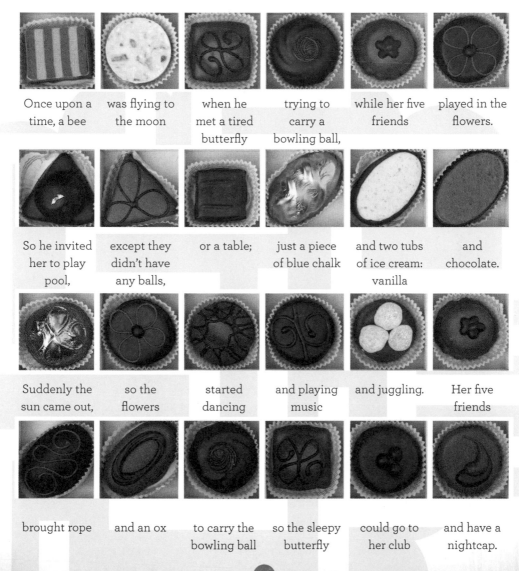

Once upon a time, a bee	was flying to the moon	when he met a tired butterfly	trying to carry a bowling ball,	while her five friends	played in the flowers.
So he invited her to play pool,	except they didn't have any balls,	or a table;	just a piece of blue chalk	and two tubs of ice cream: vanilla	and chocolate.
Suddenly the sun came out,	so the flowers	started dancing	and playing music	and juggling.	Her five friends
brought rope	and an ox	to carry the bowling ball	so the sleepy butterfly	could go to her club	and have a nightcap.

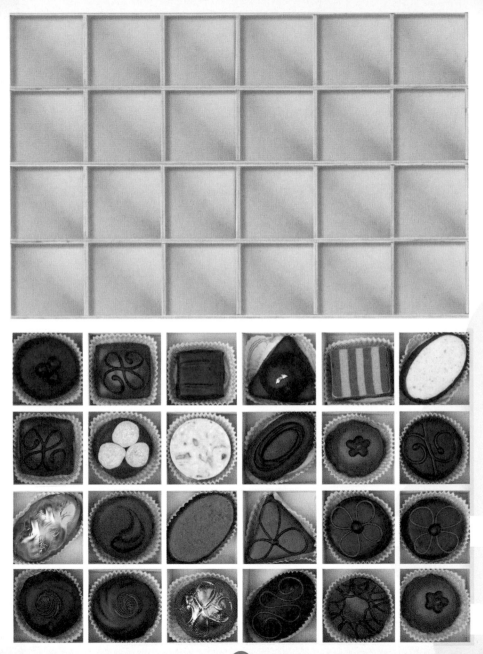

OBJECT RECALL

How good are you at remembering objects? Here's a visual memory test similar to the one on page 17. Spend one minute looking at the picture below, then turn the page and answer questions 1 and 2.

How did you get on? Did you find it harder to figure out what objects were missing because they had been jumbled around? This is because we don't remember objects in isolation but in patterns and groups, in relationship to each other.

Most people find it easier to remember the missing knife, green boot, and candle than the scissors and newspaper, because the first three are all part of a set. However, you probably wouldn't have noticed there was an orange missing unless you had taken the trouble to count them. So grouping and patterns help us to remember objects, but when we look at a group of objects, our ability to "subitize" (know immediately how many items there are at a glance) is quite low, about four, unless the items are arranged in familiar shapes.

1. How many objects have been removed?

2. Name the missing objects.

Now turn back to the previous page.

Now study this picture for two minutes. Then turn the page and answer questions 3 and 4.

How did you get on this time? There were eight items missing (rather than six) and yet you were probably able to recall all of them because they were all fruit or berries. Once you recognized that a whole category of items had vanished, you could use your semantic memory of fruit and berries to prompt you. Instead of trying to remember what was missing, you could come at the problem from the other side, running through the fruit and berry items in your semantic memory to check if they had been in the picture.

CATEGORIZE AND LOOK FOR PATTERNS

To memorize a group of objects, look for patterns and semantic relationships between them, because you can't always rely on the spatial arrangement to help you, since that is subject to change, whereas semantic patterns rarely change.

THE PARTHENON OBJECT EXPERIMENT

This phenomenon of grouping objects together spatially also works outdoors on a grand scale. A team led by Timothy McNamara, Professor of Psychology at Vanderbilt University, conducted a study to demonstrate how orientation of the viewer and the surrounding area impacts memory for object locations.

The study took place in Centennial Park in Nashville, Tennessee, where stands a full-scale replica of the Parthenon, the ancient temple on the Athenian Acropolis in Greece. Participants were blindfolded and taken to the park. Their blindfolds were then removed and they were led to one of two paths along which they walked and had to memorize eight objects located along their route. The first path was a rectangle whose sides matched the orientation of the Parthenon; the other path was at 45 degrees to it. The objects were located at the intersections of the two paths. The participants who had walked on the first path had significantly better recall of the relative location of the objects than those who had walked on the misaligned path. They had used the largest object in the vicinity—the Parthenon—for spatial orientation as a frame of reference for the other eight objects.

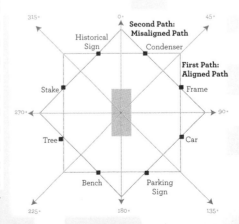

3. How many objects have been removed?

4. Name the missing objects.

Now turn back to the previous page.

HOW DOES CULTURE SHAPE MEMORY?

Write down the first five things that you can remember about your last birthday party.

What did you include in your list? The color of the cake, the gifts you received, the food you ate, or was it the people who were there? According to a recent U.S. study, this depends on your culture. Americans tend to focus on visual details—such as the color of the decorations or the type of frosting on the cake. East Asians in the study would have better remembered interpersonal details–who cut the cake or the people present.

Angela Gutchess, assistant professor of psychology at Brandeis University, and her team performed a series of memory tests on 65 students from the United States and East Asian countries, including China, Japan, and Korea.

Both groups of students scored similarly on general memory tests but the Americans were better at object recall.

"Your culture influences what you perceive to be important around you," explains Angela Gutchess. "If your culture values social interactions, you will remember those interactions better than a culture that values individual perceptions. Culture really shapes your memory."

MEMORY HOOK
NUMBER SHAPE

A hook is a mental coat hook on which you hang the information you want to commit to memory. It's an effective way to remember a group of items such as a shopping list and in a specific order.

First you must associate each number with one memorable object that closely resembles the written form. Converting abstract data into pictures makes them easier to remember. Here are some examples, but feel free to devise your own:

1 = candle   **2** = swan   **3** = heart   **4** = sail of a yacht   **5** = hook

6 = elephant's trunk   **7** = ax   **8** = hourglass   **9** = balloon on a string   **10** = doughnut

| 1 | 2 | 3 | 4 | 5 | 6 | 7 | 8 | 9 | 10 |

Now take your shopping list and associate a number image with each item to form a memorable tableau, the crazier the better.

1. **Bread:** Candle sandwich—imagine biting into it
2. **Cheese:** Swan swimming in a lake of melted cheese
3. **Baked beans:** Baked bean can being carried by a butler on a red velvet heart cushion
4. **Peanut butter:** Yacht sail smeared with peanut butter
5. **Apples:** Big green apple with a hook in it
6. **Olive oil:** Elephant in a health spa having a hot oil massage
7. **Carrots:** Paula Dean chopping carrots with an ax
8. **Chips:** Potato chips flowing like sand through a giant hourglass
9. **Ice cream:** Child carrying a balloon and an ice cream
10. **Dishwasher tablets:** A dishwasher filled with doughnuts

To recall the items, just think of each number image one at a time (candle, swan, heart, etc.) and the associated item on your shopping list (bread, cheese, baked beans) will spring back into your mind!

TOP TEN STARTING MLB PITCHERS EVER

1. Walter Johnson	6. Greg Maddux
2. Nolan Ryan	7. Bob Feller
3. Roger Clemens	8. Tom Seaver
4. Cy Young	9. Christy Mathewson
5. Warren Spahn	10. Sandy Koufax

You can memorize this list by associating a number image with each pitcher to form a memorable tableau. If you can visualize the faces of these men or you know something about them, you'll have an easier task because you only have to associate the face or another piece of your knowledge with the number shape (e.g. Walter Johnson holding a candle, Nolan Ryan riding a swan, Roger Clemens making a heart sign with his hands, etc.).

However, if you aren't a sports fan and these guys are just names to you, then you'll also need to devise a familiar image to help you recall the name or part of the name:

1. **Walter Johnson: Walter** White (from *Breaking Bad*) gives a **candle** to Magic **Johnson**

2. **Nolan Ryan: Batman** (directed by Christopher **Nolan**) rescues **Ryan** Seacrest who is being attacked by a **swan**

3. **Roger Clemens:** A jolly-**roger** flag-waving pirate sends a **heart**-shaped Valentine's card to **Clem** (the peaceful Loose-Skinned Demon from *Buffy the Vampire Slayer*)

ONCE UPON A HOOK

Imagine you had to memorize the 13 original colonies, in the order in which they joined the Union. This storytelling game is a great way to have fun and learn a list at the same time.

Take turns to tell a silly story, which links the items together and shoehorns your number images in the most implausible way for maximum comic effect. You might begin, "Once upon a hook, Richard Branson (**Virgin**ia) balancing a **candle** on his head was having a tea party (Boston, **Massachusetts**) with Marcel Proust (**Swan's** Way) when he sat on a huge granite teapot (Granite State, **New Hampshire**) and had a **heart** attack…" If your partner doesn't understand any of the linking references, s/he challenges and you must explain yourself. This helps you to build up multiple associations, which will embed the items and their order firmly in your memories.

MEMORY HOOK
NUMBER RHYME

This is very similar to the number shape system but instead you associate each number with one memorable object that rhymes with the spoken form. This method uses both the visual and the auditory memory and is an effective way to remember a group of items.

Begin by pairing each number with a rhyming memorable object. Here are some examples, but feel free to devise your own (use the first word that springs into your mind).

1 = wand   **2** = shoe   **3** = tree   **4** = door   **5** = hive

6 = sticks   **7** = heaven   **8** = crate   **9** = wine   **10** = hen

| 1 | 2 | 3 | 4 | 5 | 6 | 7 | 8 | 9 | 10 |

Now take your shopping list and associate a number image with each item to form a memorable tableau, the crazier the better.

1. **Bread:** Loaf of bread with a wand sticking out of it
2. **Cheese:** Smelly shoe stinks of cheese, with flies and smoke coming out of it
3. **Baked beans:** Tree with baked bean cans growing on it
4. **Peanut butter:** Door with peanut butter smeared on the handle
5. **Apples:** Apple stuffed into the entrance of a beehive, angry bees
6. **Olive oil:** Dipping sticks into olive oil and eating them like bread sticks
7. **Carrots:** A carrot sitting on a cloud
8. **Chips:** A huge crate filled with potato chips
9. **Ice cream:** Ice cream floating in a glass of wine
10. **Dishwasher tablets:** A hen sitting inside the dishwasher

To recall the items, just think of each number image in turn (wand, shoe, tree, etc.) and the associated item on your shopping list (bread, cheese, baked beans) will spring back into your mind!

THE RANKING OF POKER HANDS

1. Royal flush   2. Straight flush   3. Four of a kind   4. Full house   5. Flush
6. Straight   7. Three of a kind   8. Two pairs   9. One pair   10. High card

You can memorize this list by associating a number rhyme image with each hand to form a memorable tableau.

1. **Royal flush:** King Henry VIII flushing a wand down the toilet
2. **Straight flush:** Country star George Strait flushing his shoe down the toilet
3. **Four of a kind:** A square garden with a tree planted at each corner
4. **Full house:** A house filled with doors
5. **Flush:** Flushing a hive down the toilet
6. **Straight:** George Strait with some sticks
7. **Three of a kind:** Three clouds forming a triangle
8. **Two pairs:** A crate with two pears in it
9. **One pair:** A pear sitting in a wine glass
10. **High card:** A hen doing the high jump

Notice how you can use George Strait twice, and do lots of toilet flushing without confusion because the number rhyme image takes care of the order of the items in the list, and the other details help you remember the details of the list. The "four of a kind" and "three of a kind" required some additional mental imagery to help you remember the numbers within the item by forming a shape with your number rhyme images.

NOW USE THIS MEMORY TECHNIQUE
TO MEMORIZE THIS LIST:

1. Iceland   2. Norway   3. Denmark   4. Finland   5. Austria
6. Switzerland   7. New Zealand   8. Sweden   9. Singapore   10. Canada

Do you know what this list represents? (*see* page 143 for answer).

MEMORY HOOK
ALPHABET

This is similar to the number shape and number rhyme systems on the earlier pages, only this system involves the entire alphabet, allowing you to remember longer lists.

First you must associate each letter of the alphabet with an object. There are two ways to do this, either by sounds or by using concrete words.

Here is an example of each kind of alphabet, but feel free to devise your own (use the first word that springs into your mind):

Sound	Concrete	Sound	Concrete
A = hay	A = apple	N = hen	N = ninja
B = bee	B = ball	O = hoe	O = orange
C = sea	C = cat	P = pea	P = panda
D = deer	D = duck	Q = cue	Q = queen
E = knee	E = elephant	R = oar	R = rat
F = effort	F = frog	S = ass	S = sugar
G = jeans	G = grapes	T = tea	T = tent
H = age	H = hen	U = ewe	U = umbrella
I = eye	I = igloo	V = veal	V = violin
J = jay	J = jelly	W = bubble	W = whale
K = key	K = kangaroo	X = eggs	X = xylophone
L = elbow	L = lamp	Y = wire	Y = yoyo
M = hem	M = mouse	Z = zen	Z = zebra

HERE IS A SHOPPING LIST WITH 25 ITEMS:

beef	eggs	fish	yogurt	cheese
potatoes	lettuce	tomato	cucumber	cookies
sugar	bread	soup	ketchup	meatballs
toothpaste	coleslaw	hummus	corn	bananas
gravy	apples	pizza	cauliflower	broccoli

To remember the list, associate the first item on the list with hay or apple (depending on which kind of alphabet you choose), the second item with a bee or ball, etc. You don't have to create a story, just make a strong association between the alphabet words and the groceries.

To recall the items, go through the alphabet letter by letter, recall the letter word, and the associated grocery item will come back into your mind. For example, picture beef wrapped in hay, a bee juggling with eggs, fish swimming in the sea, a deer with a yogurt container on its antlers, you with knees made out of cheese (rhymes as well!), and so on.

Don't spend too long creating these images; just think them up and move on to the next item on the list.

Go through all 25 items now and make an association as described. This should take you about three minutes.

Now close your eyes and run through the alphabet and you will be amazed how much you have retained. You should be able to remember 80 percent. By this time next week you will have forgotten it (without rehearsal), but you only need to retain the items in your memory long enough for you to reach the supermarket.

There are 35 objects on this page. Spend five minutes methodically going through the alphabet to create an association between each letter-word and object. When you reach "Z," start again at "A" and link a second object with your first image (so you'll have a pair of objects for the first nine letters of the alphabet). Then close the book and run through the alphabet, writing down as many objects as you can remember. *See* page 143 for your assessment.

MEMORY PALACE

This is the mother lode of visual memory techniques. It is used by professional mnemonists like eight-time World Memory Champion Dominic O'Brien to achieve world record feats of memory, but it is actually more than 2,000 years old and can easily be learned and used by anyone.

The earliest recorded reference to the "method of loci" (*locus* is Latin for "place") appears in ancient Roman and Greek writings, including the anonymous *Rhetorica ad Herennium*, Cicero's *De Oratore*, and Quintilian's *Institutio Oratoria*, which all date back to the first century BC. In Roman culture, orators were expected to speak without using notes, so the method of loci was very popular.

Its strength is based on visual-spatial and episodic memory and the fact that it is completely personal. The memory palaces that you create are unique because everybody has an internal spatial memory map representing their version of the outside world. Even if you think that your memory is weak, you will still be able to close your eyes and mentally walk through your house or other familiar locations noticing many of the objects that populate them.

You already have this wonderful three-dimensional matrix of memory hooks stored in your brain—that's your memory palace. To memorize a list of items, all you have to do is plan a route through it and then associate the objects that you want to remember with specific objects and locations (hook points) in your memory palace.

CHOOSE AND PREPARE YOUR MEMORY PALACE

Before you start memorizing, you must plan the route so that you can repeat the same journey every time without missing out any of the hook points. The best way to do this is by memory, rather than actually walking the route, because you need to work with what is already in your long-term memory. There is no limit to how many hook points you create. You might choose one per room or ten—it doesn't matter, so long as each one is distinct and you can repeat the journey accurately without leaving any out.

ASSOCIATE YOUR ITEMS

Mentally walk around your memory palace placing the items you want to remember at your hook points. Really make them interact with the environment. Suppose one of the things you had to remember was a dental appointment and your hook point was a lamp in the corner of your living room; you could place your dentist in the corner, holding the lamp. Make the images fun because your brain likes fun. If you want to remember bacon on a list of groceries, don't just place a package of bacon in your hook point—have hundreds of slices of bacon and drape them all over the hook point. If the hook point is your television, stick slimy bacon all over the screen, stuff bacon into the speakers, pile bacon on top until you have a baconTV—object and hook point totally integrated.

Bizarre images are easier to remember than common material (this is known as the "Von Restorff effect" or "isolation effect") but the most important factor is to establish a strong link between image and hook point. To recall your items, simply retrace your steps and perform the exact same journey.

Establish your memory palace *first* and then test run it by committing these 25 items to memory. If you forget any items it will either be because your route or hook points are not firmly established, or because you didn't make the object interact strongly enough with the environment.

MEMORY LINK SYSTEM

The story of the wasp and the butterfly that helped you to remember the 24 chocolates on page 81 is an example of a memory link system.

This simple method involves using images to link, in a sequence, all the items that you want to commit to memory. They don't have to tell a story, but you might find that this happens naturally anyway. The plot of the story or tableau doesn't have to follow any of the normal rules of storytelling; it is created solely to link the images in the most memorable way. The images can be purely visual or they could have a phonetic/auditory component (like the lettuce below).

The planet Jupiter has over 65 moons. Suppose you wanted to learn the first ten in order by their distance from Jupiter: Metis, Adrastea, Amalthea, Thebe, Io, Europa, Ganymede, Callisto, Leda, Himalia.

You could do this using either the basic link method or the story link method. They are slightly more labor-intensive than other mnemonics, so they are most suited to memorizing facts that are unlikely to change and that you want to remember forever (as opposed to a shopping list, which is redundant as soon as you've been shopping).

REMEMBERING WITH THE LINK METHOD

- A LETTUCE with an M on it (**Metis**) has a DRASTIC TEAR in it (**Adrastea**)
- The DRASTIC TEAR was made by a MOUSE with a LISP (**Amalthea**)
- SLEEPY (**Thebe**) is one of the Seven Dwarfs who sings "IO, it's off to work we go to Europe" (**Io, Europa**)
- In Europe everyone drinks MEAD (**Ganymede**)
- MEAD makes Calista Flockhart (**Callisto**) tipsy, so she asks Harrison Ford to LEAD HER (**Leda**) to the HIMALAYAS (**Himalia**) to sober up

The story link method is very similar, but has more of a narrative structure.

REMEMBERING WITH THE STORY LINK METHOD

A LETTUCE with an M on it (**Metis**) had a DRASTIC TEAR (**Adrastea**) because a LISPING MOUSE (**Amalthea**) accidentally stepped on it as he was SLEEPILY (**Thebe**) singing "IO, it's off to work we go" (**Io**) while on his way to EUROPE (**Europa**) where he hoped to find everyone was drinking MEAD (**Ganymede**), especially his favorite actress Calista Flockhart (**Callisto**), who was so drunk that she asked husband Harrison Ford to LEAD HER (**Leda**) to the HIMALAYAS (**Himalia**) to sober up in the fresh air.

Here are some more lists that are well suited to the memory link method. Alternatively, you could use the acronym method on page 103, the number shape memory hook (*see* page 89) or the number rhyme memory hook (*see* page 91). Use whichever works best for you, but experiment with all of them.

TUDOR MONARCHS OF ENGLAND AND IRELAND

Henry VII , Henry VIII, Edward VI, Lady Jane Grey, Mary I, Elizabeth I

THE FIRST TEN U.S. PRESIDENTS

George Washington, John Adams, Thomas Jefferson, James Madison, James Monroe, John Quincy Adams, Andrew Jackson, Martin Van Buren, William Henry Harrison, John Tyler

THE FIRST TEN AMENDMENTS TO THE U.S. CONSTITUTION

1. freedom of religion, speech, press and assembly; right of petition

2. right to bear arms

3. limit on quartering of troops

4. protection against unreasonable search and seizure

5. due process, double jeopardy; self-incrimination

6. right to speedy trial

7. trial by jury in civil cases

8. no excessive bail or fine; no cruel or unusual punishment

9. people retain rights

10. powers not delegated to the U.S. states or people

MNEMONICS
AND ACRONYMS

A MNEMONIC IS ANY METHOD OR DEVICE THAT HELPS MEMORY. HERE ARE SOME EXAMPLES OF VERBAL MNEMONICS, NUMERICAL MNEMONICS, AND ACRONYMS.

VERBAL MNEMONICS

1. Colors of the rainbow in order:
   red, orange, yellow, green, blue, indigo, violet

   Richard Of York Gave Battle In Vain

2. Color codes used in electronics, in numerical order:
   black (0), brown (1), red (2), orange (3), yellow (4), green (5), blue (6), violet or purple (7), gray (8), and white (9)

   Bill Brown Realized Only Yesterday Good Boys Value Good Work

3. Names of the planets:
   Mercury, Venus, Earth, Mars, Jupiter, Saturn, Uranus, Neptune

   My Very Educated Mother Just Served Us Nachos

4. The notes on the spaces on the bass clef stave:
   A, C, E, G

   All Cows Eat Grass

5. Order of Mohs hardness scale from 1 to 10:
   Talc, Gypsum, Calcite, Fluorite, Apatite, Orthoclase feldspar, Quartz, Topaz, Corundum, Diamond

   Toronto Girls Can Flirt, And Other Queer Things Can Do

6. The first eight U.S. presidents:
   George Washington, John Adams, Thomas Jefferson, James Madison, James Monroe, John Quincy Adams, Andrew Jackson, Martin Van Buren

   Will A Jolly Man Make A Jolly Visitor?

7. How to spell POTASSIUM:

   one **t**ea, two **s**ugars

8. When to use the spellings "stationery" and "stationary":

   There is an "e" in envelope = station**e**ry

9. The royal houses of England:
   Norman, Plantagenet, Lancaster, York, Tudor, Stuart, Hanover, Windsor

   No Planes Landed Yesterday, Ten Stewardesses Have Warts

10. Order of geological time periods:
    Cambrian, Ordovician, Silurian, Devonian, Carboniferous, Permian, Triassic, Jurassic, Cretaceous, Paleocene, Eocene, Oligocene, Miocene, Pliocene, Pleistocene, Recent

    Camels Often Sit Down Carefully. Perhaps Their Joints Creak? Persistent Early Oiling Might Prevent Painful Rheumatism.

11. The notes on the lines on the treble clef stave:
    E, G, B, D, F

    Every Good Boy Deserves Fruit

12. Reactivity of metals:
    Potassium, Sodium, Calcium, Magnesium, Aluminum, Zinc, Iron, Lead, Copper, Mercury, Silver, Platinum

    Please Send Cats, Monkeys And Zebras In Large Cages Make Sure Padlocked

13. The notes on the lines on the bass clef stave:
    G, B, D, F, A

    Good Boys Deserve Fruit Always

14. Order of biological classification:
    Kingdom, Phylum, Class, Order, Family, Genus, Species

    King Philip Came Over For Great Soup

15. Bactrian camel has two humps, Dromedary camel has one:

16. The order of operations for math:
    Parentheses, Exponents, Multiply, Divide, Add, and Subtract

    Please Excuse My Dear Aunt Sally

17. How to spell NECESSARY:

    Not Every Cat Eats Sardines (Some Are Really Yummy)

18. The eight facial bones:
    Vomer, Conchae, Nasal, Maxilla, Mandible, Palatine, Zygomatic, Lacrimal

    Virgil Can Not Make My Pet Zebra Laugh

19. The order of the earth's atmospheres:
    Troposphere, Stratosphere, Mesosphere, Thermosphere, Exosphere

    Tropical Storms Make Their Exit

20. Countries around the Adriatic Sea (in clockwise direction):
Italy, Slovenia, Croatia, Bosnia and Herzegovina, Montenegro, Albania

Incredibly Slimy Cockroach Bit My Aunt

21. Stala**g**mites are on the **g**round, stala**c**tites are on the **c**eiling.

22. What happened to the six wives of Henry VIII:

divorced, beheaded, died, divorced, beheaded, survived

23. How to spell RECEIVE:

It's better to g**ive** than rece**ive**.

24. Number of days in month:

Thirty days have September,
April, June, and November.
All the rest have 31,
Except February alone,
And that has 28 days clear,
And 29 in a leap year.

Knuckles = 31 days, hollows = 30 days (except Feb. = 28 or 29)

25. First ten chemical elements:
Hydrogen, Helium, Lithium, Beryllium, Boron, Carbon, Nitrogen, Oxygen, Fluorine, Neon

Happy Henry Likes Beer But Could Not Obtain Four Nuts

26. How to spell BELIEVE:

Do not be**lie**ve a **lie**.

27. The next eight chemical elements:
Sodium (NA), Magnesium, Aluminum, Silicon, Phosphorus, Sulfur, Chlorine, Argon

Naughty Magpies Always Sing Perfect Songs Clawing Ants

28. The 12 cranial nerves
Olfactory, Optic, Oculomotor, Trochlear, Trigeminal, Abducens, Facial, Vestibulocochlear, Glossopharyngeal, Vagus, (Spinal) Accessory, Hypoglossal.

Oh Once One Takes The Anatomy Final Very Good Vacations Are Heavenly

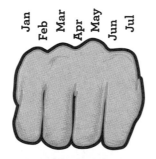

NUMERICAL/MATH MNEMONICS

1. First 15 digits of the mathematical constant pi:
   3.14159265358979

   Now I need a drink, alcoholic of course, after the heavy lectures involving quantum mechanics.

   (The number of letters in each word corresponds to a digit.)

2. The Roman numerals 50, 100, 500, 1000:

   Lazy Cats Don't Move (L, C, D, M)

3. Sine = Opposite over Hypotenuse;
   Cosine = Adjacent over Hypotenuse; and
   Tangent = Opposite over Adjacent

   SOH-CAH-TOA

   (Sine, Cosine and Tangent are trigonometric functions which relate the angles of a right-angled triangle to the lengths of its sides.)

4. Speed of light in meters per second:
   299,792,458

   We guarantee certainty, clearly referring to this light mnemonic.
   (The number of letters in each word corresponds to a digit.)

5. Three basic trigonometry relationships in triangles:
   Opposite = Adjacent x $\text{Tan}\theta$;
   Adjacent = Hypotenuse x $\text{Cos}\theta$;
   Opposite = Hypotenuse x $\text{Sin}\theta$

   Old Aunt Tabatha, And Her Cat, On Her Ship

   (Sine, Cosine, and Tangent are trigonometric functions which relate the angles of a right-angled triangle to the lengths of its sides.)

ACRONYMS

1. The colors of the rainbow in order:
   Red, Orange, Yellow, Green, Blue, Indigo, Violet

   ROY G. BIV

2. The position of the North American Great Lakes on a map:
   Superior, Huron, Ontario, Michigan, Erie

   SHO ME

3. In English, the eight parts of speech:
   Pronouns, Adjectives, Verbs, Prepositions, Adverbs, Nouns, Interjections, Conjunctions

   PAVPANIC

4. Scuba diving predive safety checklist:
   Buoyancy, Weights, Releases, Air, Final check

   BW RAF

5. The notes on the spaces on the treble clef stave:

    FACE

6. In English, the seven coordinating conjunctions:
    For, And, Nor, But, Or, Yet, So

    FANBOYS

7. The most salient interrelated factors that explain the decline of a civilization:
    Water, Energy, Climate, Agriculture, Population

    WECAP

8. The stages of cell division:
    Interphase, Prophase, Metaphase, Anaphase, Telephase

    IPMAT

9. The order of operations for math:
    Parentheses, Exponents, Multiply, Divide, Add or Subtract

    PEMDAS

10. Seven deadly sins:
    Pride, Avarice (greed), Lust, Envy, Gluttony, Anger (wrath), Sloth

    PALE GAS

ACROSTICS

An acrostic is a form of writing, usually a poem, which contains a secret word or message, spelled out with the initial, final, or another chosen letter of each line, sentence, or paragraph. The word "acrostic" comes from combining the Greek words ἄκρος (extreme) and στίχος (line/verse). Acrostics can be used for encryption or as powerful mnemonics (devices to aid memory retrieval); they are a great way to invent passwords you'll never forget (because you've already learned them).

Acrostics have been around for millennia and were particularly popular with the Greeks of the Alexandrine period, the poets of the Italian Renaissance, and the Elizabethans. The first printed version that survives of an acrostic poem is "The Strife of Love in a Dream," written at the end of the fifteenth century by a smitten monk to record his clandestine love for a woman. The initial letters of the first words of each section spell out in Latin the message, "Brother Francis Colonna passionately loves Polia."

Acrostics also feature in the Hebrew Bible and the Greek exclamation "Ἰησούς Χριστός, Θεού Υιός, Σωτήρ; Iesous CHristos, THeou Yios, Soter" (Jesus Christ, God's son, savior) spells out ICHTHYS (ΙΧΘΥΣ), Greek for fish. Christians adopted this as their secret symbol to avoid persecution by the Roman Empire.

One of the most famous ancient acrostics is the 25-letter Roman "Sator Square" (see right).

The earliest datable square was discovered in the ruins of Pompeii, but many others have been found in locations around the world, including Cirencester in England, beneath the church of Santa Maria Maggiore in Rome, and in Syria.

S	A	T	O	R
A	R	E	P	O
T	E	N	E	T
O	P	E	R	A
R	O	T	A	S

It reads the same upward, downward, backward, and forward. It appears in a lot of occult literature and records of medieval magic, because of its unique symmetry. It means "The farmer Arepo holds wheels for work" or "The farmer uses his plow to work."

Acrostics make convenient passwords—you can create one by taking the initial or final letters of words of a song that you already know. For instance, this password was created by taking the initial letters of words in the first two lines of a famous Elton John hit: gNJtinkyaa.

It's "Candle in the Wind" (the original version). Everyone has a unique catalog of favorite song lyrics stored in their long-term memory, so using them to create acrostic passwords is easy because you've already memorized them. If you want to keep track of which songs you've used, simply create a playlist or write a list of songs. Anyone seeing it won't realize that it's highly sensitive information.

Here's an example of an acrostic poem, by Edgar Allan Poe. Its title and the first word are a giveaway:

AN ACROSTIC
by Edgar Allan Poe (written c. 1829)

Elizabeth it is in vain you say

"Love not"—thou sayest it in so sweet a way:

In vain those words from thee or L. E. L.

Zantippe's talents had enforced so well:

Ah! if that language from thy heart arise,

Breathe it less gently forth—and veil thine eyes.

Endymion, recollect, when Luna tried

To cure his love—was cured of all beside—

His folly—pride—and passion—for he died.

ACROSTIC PASSWORDS

Here is a list of 12 initial letter acrostic passwords; see if you can crack them. The only clue is the artist.

nfnfwkhtdi (Bee Gees), bymiwtl (Johnny Cash), gsiybwgpliyb (50 Cent), ittrlitjfcialnefr (Queen), wwwmwdifltigcn (Rihanna), latslhtsfy (Coldplay), hygciyc (Arctic Monkeys), Lcttftnwidabcd (The Clash), yanbahdcatt (Elvis Presley), inmtcyasinmtcyap (Prince), icfyhhhicsyhhh (Beyoncé), haisimtcfatM (David Bowie)

REMEMBER
NAMES AND FACES

If you are hopeless at remembering names and faces, don't worry, you're not alone. In fact, studies have shown that most people find it harder to remember a name than an occupation and other biographical details, which hold more interest and meaning so they are easier to remember. Most of us don't have any trouble recalling a face (although as many as 2.5 percent of the population suffer from prosopagnosia—genetic face blindness).

A name is just an abstract label, so unless you use imagery to make names concrete, you will always struggle to remember them, like the vast majority of the general population.

1. Pay attention and don't get distracted. When you are being introduced to someone for the first time, concentrate on listening and remembering their name rather than getting so distracted by all the social niceties—handshaking, cheek kissing, smiling, trying to look interesting and/or interested—that you don't listen properly.

2. If you don't listen properly or don't catch the name, ask for it to be repeated. It's better to do this immediately than have to spend an entire conversation hoping you aren't going to have to introduce them to anyone else.

3. Try to link the name with a concrete image. If the person's name is Jerry, that might remind you of jelly, so link Jerry with the jelly—imagine it smeared all over his face, or that a jar of jelly is stuck on top of his head.

4. Identify the person's most distinctive feature—big nose, recessive chin, freckles—and link your image to this feature. If Jerry has big ears that stick out, imagine spreading strawberry jelly on them before sticking them to the side of his face.

5. Introduce the name at least once into a conversation (any more than this might appear insincere).

6. After the initial encounter has finished, spend a few minutes consolidating in your memory the names of people you have just met. This brief recap will deepen the encoding.

7. Don't smoke. Studies show that nonsmokers remember names and faces better than smokers.

USING THE STRATEGIES YOU HAVE JUST LEARNED, SPEND TEN MINUTES MEMORIZING THE NAMES OF THESE PEOPLE, THEN TURN THE PAGE AND SEE HOW MANY YOU CAN REMEMBER.

This only allows you 24 seconds for each face, to simulate what you might experience at a social gathering where you are introduced to a lot of people one after the other. So work quickly and try not to leave anyone out. If you can remember more than seven names, you are already above average, but with practice this should rise to between 15 and 25.

FACIAL RECOGNITION

The fusiform gyrus runs along the underside of the temporal and occipital lobes of the brain, across both hemispheres—although it is larger in the right side. This area of the brain deals with facial recognition and it also communicates with the occipital lobe, where visual input is processed. Damage to the fusiform gyrus or to the neural pathways that lead from it to the occipital lobe usually results in impaired facial recognition, even of family and friends.

The facial recognition system, like language acquisition, becomes specialized as children grow older. Just as the ability to learn a foreign language like a native speaker drops off in infancy, recognizing faces from other ethnic groups also declines without regular exposure. We find it easier to recognize faces from our own culture, so growing up in a multicultural environment has lasting benefits for facial recognition abilities in later life.

Studies have also shown gender differences in face recognition. Men tend to recognize fewer female faces than women do, but there are no gender differences associated with male faces.

Facial recognition also has an emotional memory component, because when we see a face, we need to recall how we feel about that person and assess whether they are an ally or a threat. Damage to this system (e.g. a communication failure between the temporal cortex, which processes faces, and the limbic system, which deals with emotion) can lead to a condition called Capgras syndrome (or the Capgras Delusion), in which a person is convinced that a friend or relative has been replaced by an identical-looking imposter. Imagine recognizing your mother, but without any of the emotions that you would expect to feel; it's easy to see how this could lead you to think that something about her was "off."

If you can remember half of the names, very well done. As you can see, it's a challenge, but with practice you will be able to speed up the process (which is essential) and improve your hit rate in busy social situations.

USING BOTH SIDES
OF THE BRAIN

Since the 1960s, popular psychology has propagated the concept of "left-brained" and "right-brained" personalities. You are probably familiar with the idea that right-brained people are creative, impulsive, intuitive, imaginative, and subjective, while left-brainers are analytical, attentive, detail-oriented, objective, and rational. In fact our brains are much more sophisticated than this. However, the concept can still be used to help you highlight some of your broad personality traits since they have a direct impact on how best you learn. It is important to recognize what kind of learner you are so you can adapt your learning style and/or work on your weaknesses. Fortunately, the brain is remarkably malleable even into late adulthood, so if you are impulsive, risk-taking, and big-picture oriented by nature, you can learn to be more logical, risk-aware, and detail-oriented (and vice versa).

COMMON CHARACTERISTICS OF A LEFT-BRAIN LEARNER

Memorizes best by repetition (auditory or writing)

Has no difficulty processing information that is presented verbally

Likes structure, making plans, timetables, routine

Prefers to work alone in a quiet environment

Happy with a lecture format (being talked at)

Can learn without requiring an emotional attachment to the material

COMMON CHARACTERISTICS OF A RIGHT-BRAIN LEARNER

Memorizes best by using meaning, color, pictures, story, or emotion in material

May have difficulty processing information that is presented verbally; needs visual input

Does not plan ahead regularly, likes to keep options open

Prefers to work in a group in a busy, even noisy environment

Prefers hands-on activities (doing) over a lecture format

Needs to feel emotionally involved with the material

ARE YOU RIGHT- OR LEFT-BRAINED?

1. Draw a Q on your forehead with your finger. Which direction did you draw the tail?

   a. Pointing toward your finger
   b. Pointing away from your finger

2. What does your desk/bedroom look like?

   a. Tidy
   b. Cluttered

3. If you could choose an assignment topic, would you rather:

   a. Describe the planets in the solar system
   b. Write a story about a flea that saves the world

4. I base important decisions on:

   a. Logic
   b. Intuition

5. I am a risk-taker.

   a. No
   b. Yes

6. It is easier for me to remember faces than names.

   a. No
   b. Yes

7. There is a right and a wrong way to do everything.

   a. Yes
   b. No

8. I am usually on time for my appointments.

   a. Yes
   b. No

9. If I lost something, I'd try to remember where I saw it last.

   a. No
   b. Yes

10. If I had to assemble something, I'd read the directions first.

    a. Yes
    b. No

RESULTS

Mostly (A): You are left-brained

Mostly (B): You are right-brained

Roughly equal (A) and (B): You do not have a dominant side and have attributes of both.

HOW TO MINIMIZE
MEMORY LOSS

As already discussed, the best way to improve your memory is to stay healthy by exercising regularly, getting plenty of sleep, eating healthy food, and keeping your brain active by doing memory exercises. However, several other lifestyle factors affect your mental and physical well-being and, with it, your memory.

POSITIVE SOCIAL INTERACTION

Surround yourself with friends and family and cultivate an active social life. Older people who maintain close ties with others have better mental performance than those who are more isolated. Social interaction stimulates the brain, but it is important to associate with people who encourage and make you feel good and allow you to self-actualize.

Scientists have studied how relationships can affect cognitive performance. In one study, nursing home residents were asked to complete a jigsaw. One group was given verbal encouragement, a second group was actively shown where the pieces fitted, and the third group was given no support. Later, they all attempted another puzzle independently. The people in the group that had been encouraged (while remaining independent) improved their performance; the second group performed worse; and those who had received no support remained the same.

STOP SMOKING

Smoking constricts the arteries, damages the lungs, and increases the risk of high blood pressure and stroke, all of which reduce oxygen flow to the brain, which affects memory.

CHALLENGE YOUR BRAIN WITH NEW EXPERIENCES

Your brain thrives on new input, new sights, sounds, and smells, breaks in routine, and interesting novel experiences. Variety isn't just the spice of life, it's also a memory booster—cross-training for mind and body.

CHECK YOUR MEDICATION

If you take medication to reduce anxiety, help you sleep, or treat allergies, it could affect your memory. Dr. Cara Tannenbaum, research chair at the Montreal Geriatric University Institute and associate professor of medicine and pharmacy at the University of Montreal, has found a link between certain kinds of medication and memory issues, including benzodiazepines (used to treat anxiety and insomnia), antihistamines, and tricyclic antidepressants. Don't stop taking your meds, but do discuss any memory concerns with your doctor.

SEEK HELP FOR DEPRESSION

If you think you might be suffering from depression, seek help. It has long been known that depression weakens the memory. Recent research by Brigham Young University published in the journal *Behavioural Brain Research*, indicates that depression impairs the ability to distinguish between things that are similar, a skill called "pattern separation." The more depressed a person is, the harder it becomes for them to differentiate similar experiences they have had.

Depressed people don't have amnesia as such, they are just missing the details, which impairs their ability to form long-term memories. One of the physical effects of depression is a measurable decrease in the growth of new brain cells in the hippocampus, a crucial part of the brain involved in memory formation and storage.

TAKE UP A CRAFT HOBBY

Researchers from the Mayo Clinic in Minnesota compared nearly 200 people aged 70 to 89 with mild memory problems, with a group with no impairment. Those who had read books, played games, enjoyed puzzles and crosswords, or pursued a craft hobby such as knitting or quilting had a 40 percent reduced risk of memory impairment.

REDUCE SUGAR IN YOUR DIET

A recent UCLA study with rats, published in the *Journal of Physiology*, showed a link between a diet high in fructose and memory and learning impairment. Fernando Gomez-Pinilla, a professor of neurosurgery at the David Geffen School of Medicine at UCLA, says, "Eating a high-fructose diet over the long term alters your brain's ability to learn and remember information. But adding omega-3 fatty acids to your meals can help minimize the damage."

MIND MAPPING

Creating a mind map is an effective way to visualize and organize ideas and create a network of associations. This also makes it an ideal way to encode and test your recall of factual information from your declarative memory (*see* page 45).

A mind map usually consists of a single word or idea, placed in the center of a page. Ideas and related information are then added, branching out from the center. This creates a page of information that is nonlinear, free from Western sinistrodextral (left-to-right) word formation. You can also use different colored ink to categorize information visually.

Mind maps can also help you to understand concepts, which is an important first step in memorizing; it's very hard to learn something that you don't properly understand, so if you are struggling to learn and understand information, write it down as a mind map.

Before you learn how to create a mind map, here are three important details to remember:

- They should only contain keywords and short phrases. They are a way to organize ideas, not to write reams of notes.
- They encourage and strengthen associations and connections.
- They can use color, images, and symbols as well as keywords and short phrases.

HOW TO MAKE A MIND MAP

1. Start with a blank sheet of paper, at least 8 ½ x 11 inches. Turn the paper so that it is landscape oriented.

2. Write the keyword or draw the key image in the center of the page.

3. Every time you add another word or image, draw a branch from the keyword to connect with it, or draw a branch from a branch. No matter how many branches you create, it should be possible to journey back along the branches to reach the center.

4. It will also be possible to travel from one word to any other word by traveling along the branches, so everything is connected.

5. Draw curved branches, not straight lines. Curves are more organic and flowing and encourage creative thinking; straight lines may encourage rigid thinking.

ATTENTION PLEASE

Attention is essential to effective learning. The best way to improve recall is to increase attention at the memory-forming stage. Without attention, retention is haphazard and beyond the learner's control. Attention must also target the appropriate areas of study, otherwise the retention will be strong but the information irrelevant. Effective attention involves being highly selective about what you consciously decide to commit to memory.

SEVEN WAYS TO IMPROVE YOUR ATTENTION

1. The learning task must have meaning and value, which can only be gained by understanding WHAT you are learning and WHY you are learning it.

2. Determine what is most important (see page 121).

3. Understand that attention is as much about deciding what to ignore as it is about focus. According to psychologist and philosopher William James, attention is "taking possession of the mind, in clear and vivid form, of one out of what may seem several simultaneously possible objects or trains of thoughts... It implies withdrawal from some things in order to deal effectively with others."

4. Eliminate distractions, especially those from digital media such as the television, internet, and cell phones. Psychologist Dr. Larry Rosen says that "solid research ...demonstrates how the technologies that we use daily coerce us to act in ways that may be detrimental to our well-being," causing what he calls an "iDisorder."

5. Time-limit and structure your internet activity to clearly differentiate between leisure browsing and research, so you don't waste half an hour under the pretext of "work."

6. Research has shown that self-discipline is more important than IQ in predicting academic success. Also, many people hamper their learning with the self-limiting belief that willpower is finite. In fact, studies by Stanford University psychology professors Greg Walton and Carol Dweck have shown that people who believe that willpower is unlimited and self-renewing are more effective learners than those who believe that willpower is a finite resource.

7. Reading is one of the most effective ways to increase your attention span and your attentional control—your capacity to choose what to pay attention to and what to ignore, how effectively you can engage and disengage your focus.

ATTENTION TEST

Only 20 of the symbols on these two pages look like this: 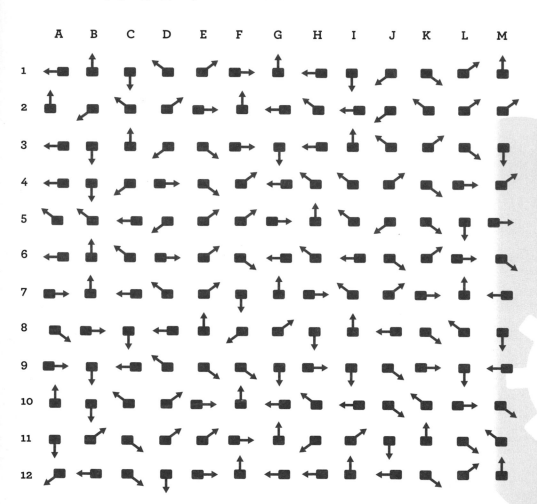. Take as long as you need but time yourself. As quickly and accurately as possible, write down the coordinates of all 20 of them. Then *see page 143-144* for your assessment.

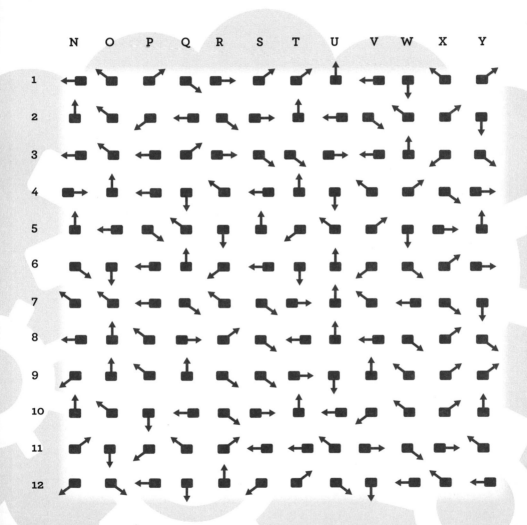

ESTABLISH REGULAR
STUDY SESSIONS

Learning is a habit, and memory works best when it can be refreshed a little every day. So it is better to study in several shorter study sessions than a single long one. You retain best what you study at the beginning and end of a session (these are known as the primacy and recency effects), so the longer the session, the less of the material you will retain in proportion to the time spent.

1. When planning six hours of study, schedule one hour every day for six days, then take a break on the seventh. If you have to learn two subjects in 12 hours, spend an hour a day on each subject for six days. This way you know that both subjects will gain the same attention.

2. Your learning will be less efficient if you split the week into two halves, focusing on one subject for half the week and the other subject for the second half of the week. Chipping away day by day at both subjects will make you feel more in control; otherwise the second subject can become a worry during the first half of the week and affect your concentration on the first subject.

3. The brain works best when it is rested. So it makes sense that each of your six study sessions spread over a week benefit from following a night's sleep (important for memory consolidation), whereas one single six-hour session only follows one night's sleep.

4. Use the Pomodoro technique to break up your study. Work for 25 minutes, take a five-minute break, work for another 25 minutes, then take another five-minute break. Every two hours, take a longer break of 25 minutes. So a two-hour study session would look like this:

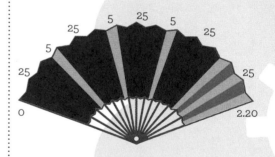

5. For every 100 minutes you spend studying, you will spend 40 minutes resting. This might seem like a lot of rest, but the gains to your attention and memory more than make up for it.

DETERMINE WHAT IS
IMPORTANT

Be highly selective about what you study. Even if your willpower is unlimited, your time is finite, so you have to be decisive about where to place your attention. Effective learners don't know everything; they just figure out what they need to learn and what they can ignore.

When you are reading a text for the first time you need to be able to judge what information is important for the meaning and understanding, and what is extraneous, even though it may be interesting. You have to make a distinction between the most and the least important information in the text otherwise everything has equal value and you will be overwhelmed.

Reading and studying is like mining rock for precious metal. Gold miners can't mine gold unless they know that this is what they are supposed to be doing. Your task is to methodically extract the nuggets of meaning. Many readers just start metaphorically hacking away at a text without a clear goal, unaware that they need to sift and select and to use high-level reasoning skills to collect the important structural and material essence.

How to mine a text for meaning, to isolate supporting details, and to read for specific information:

1. Think about facts, ideas, and your own responses while you read. Search for answers to compelling questions. Write them down.

2. Identify key ideas or themes.

3. Monitor your comprehension, so that you are aware the moment a passage stops making sense.

4. Reread anything that doesn't make sense. Don't skim over it. Rereading for sense is normal and not a sign that you are either a poor reader or stupid.

5. Look out for the structural and semantic cues that signal importance: headings, different fonts, framed text, captions, labels, lists, bullet points—all these things provide structure and point the reader toward the subtleties of meaning. Look out for key guiding words or phrases such as "for example," "however," "therefore," "in conclusion," "sometimes," "but," "never," "always," "represent the," etc.

6. Distinguish between interesting information and important information. The interesting information may be easier to learn and recall than the important information; it may also distract you from the important information. Don't let one crowd out the other in your long-term memory.

For example, say you need to learn and remember four things:

1. the etymology of the word "synapse"

2. the two basic types of synapse

3 & 4. the name and chemical structure of an important amino acid commonly associated with changes in postsynaptic signaling.

So you turn to the relevant page in your textbook and see this:

> *Comes from the Greek "synapsis" or conjunction. The word "synapse" comes from "synaptein," which Sir Charles Scott Sherrington and colleagues coined from the Greek "syn-" ("with," "together") and "haptein" ("fasten," "clasp"). There are two fundamentally different types of synapses: chemical (via the activation of voltage-gated calcium channels) and electrical (with presynaptic and postsynaptic cell membranes connected by gap junctions). The amino acid is N-methyl-D-aspartic acid receptor (NMDAR). By altering the release of neurotransmitters, plasticity of synapses can be controlled in the presynaptic cell.*

First write down the important information. This is all you need to learn:

1. "synapsis" = conjunction, *syn-* (with, together) *haptein* (to fasten, clasp)

2. chemical, electrical

3. N-methyl-d-aspartic acid receptor (NMDAR).

4.

If you struggled to extract this information, reread page 121 to check which procedures you missed. *See page 125* and how "elaborative rehearsal" can help you to commit this information to your long-term memory.

STRUCTURE AND ORGANIZE THE
INFORMATION

Organizing information and providing structure helps to package it, ready for your long-term memory. It's like sorting your groceries at the checkout into bags for the fridge, for the freezer, one for meat, another for fruit and vegetables, another for cleaning products or toiletries. When you get home you know where everything is and you can put everything in its correct place quickly and efficiently. Or you could throw it all into one hefty garbage bag and then dump it in the trunk. In both scenarios you get your groceries home, but only the first strategy is efficient and aids retrieval.

1. Group similar concepts and terms together. Use a highlighter to draw attention to important facts and ideas, then chunk them into smaller groups.

2. The "rule of three" is a popular rhetorical device used in writing and public speaking: grouping ideas together in threes to clarify meaning, give the listener structural cues, and to give a satisfying feeling of closure. Many jokes, slogans, fables, and nursery rhymes follow this triune structure, as does Winston Churchill's famous utterance after the Second Battle of El Alamein: "Now this is not the end. It is not even the beginning of the end. But it is, perhaps, the end of the beginning."

For instance, if you have highlighted 30 pieces of information, see if you can chunk this down, in a branching structure, to ten groups of three.

3. Arrange the material visually so that it can be represented in branches of information, like the mind map on page 116. This internal scaffolding and interconnectivity aid memory encoding.

Here are some more lists of information that seem impossible to remember. Impose the optimal structure to make memorizing easy (answer on page 144).

1. 589012346780124563798901567234

2. bird, calling, gold, turtle, bird, calling, gold, turtle, French, calling, gold, bird, French, calling, gold, bird, ring, dove, ring, hen, ring, dove, ring, hen, ring, hen, French, gold

3. table, knife, plate, spoon, cup, fork, jug, window, saucer, vase of flowers, cat, carrot, potato, chicken leg (hint: drawing a picture may be the best technique here)

4. Type your notes so that you can easily move text around to create the optimal structure. Use color and different fonts, to make the information more memorable.

Experiments at Princeton and Indiana Universities by **Daniel** Oppenheimer, an associate professor of psychology and public affairs at Princeton, Connor *Diemand-Yauman*, a **2010 Princeton** graduate, and Erikka **Vaughan** have shown that unusual fonts improve retention. They got one group of people to read information in 16-point Arial and others in 12-point Comic Sans MA and 12-point Bodoni MT.

The Arial font was easier to read, but it produced the worst retention.

The two fonts that were visually more challenging produced the best recall of information.

Then they conducted a bigger field trial with 222 high school students in *Chesterland,* Ohio. Some students were assigned material in three difficult fonts—**Haettenschweiler**, *Monotype Corsiva,* or **Comic Sans Italicized**—and other students were given material printed in the font that their teacher usually used, **Times New Roman** or **Arial**.

The students were tested on the material. Those who had been given hard-to-read fonts performed better than did their counterparts reading the same material in easier fonts.

The difficult fonts improve learning because of a concept called "disfluency." The reader has to concentrate harder to read the information, so retention is improved.

However, be careful that you don't use such wacky fonts that your notes become too difficult to read or even illegible. Illegible notes will not enhance your learning.

Cover the top of the page and then answer this question:

1. Write down the names of the three researchers. If you can't remember, write down your best approximation.

When you have finished, check your answers above and see if there was any connection between your retention and the choice of font. *See* answers on page 144 to see what you should have found.

ELABORATE AND
REHEARSE

Elaborative rehearsal involves taking the material and playing with it to create associations with different types of information. It means thinking about the meaning of something rather than just reading it over and over, repeating it mindlessly to yourself.

For example, say you need to learn and remember the etymology of the word "synapse," the two basic types of synapse, and the name and chemical structure of an important amino acid commonly associated with changes in postsynaptic signaling.

This is the basic important information that you mined from page 122:

1. "synapsis" = conjunction, *syn-* (with, together) *haptein* (fasten, clasp)

2. chemical, electrical

3. N-methyl-D-aspartic acid receptor (NMDAR).

4.

Committing all this information to long-term memory will be a challenge unless you elaborate to create meaningful connections. Having mined the important information from the morass of detail on page 122, the next task is to create personal scaffolding to bolt the facts into your memory. This is a highly active process (but no more time-consuming than conventional studying), that requires you to think about, reframe, and order the information in your head.

1. Think about other words you know that begin with "syn": "synthesis," "synergy," "synonym." Look them up:

   · synthesis: combination of two or more entities
   · syntax: the study of combining words to make sentences
   · synonym: words with the same or similar meanings ("with name")

Now consider "haptein":

haptics: nonverbal communication involving touch (fasten onto, touch). Your vibrating cell phone is an example of haptic technology. Now that you have made this connection with something familiar in your life, you will find it easier to remember the word "haptein" and its possible meanings more easily.

Not only have you encoded the information "syn" and "haptein," you have also increased your learning in other areas. You've ended up learning more information to support the original learning task, and deepened your interest and connectivity.

2. Chemical, electrical. This should be fairly simple to remember, because you already know that the brain experiences chemical reactions and displays electrical activity. But to reinforce the information you might imagine a chemistry flask with an electric plug inside and then quickly draw a picture of this idea.

3. **N**-**m**ethyl-**D**-**a**spartic acid **r**eceptor (NMDAR) for postsynaptic signaling.

If you learn the acronym, NMDAR, first, this will help you to remember the full name. You know it's an amino "acid" and also a "receptor," so the only words you have to learn are "methyl" and "aspartic" (the rest are letters). Simply making the effort to make these kinds of observations will make your brain pay more attention to the material.

Look up "aspartic acid" on Wikipedia and you'll see that aspartate was originally derived from asparagine, and isolated from asparagus juice. Now you have something concrete to fix your memory to: asparagus stalks.

Methyl is derived from methane. Cows produce large quantities of methane by farting and burping, so draw a picture of a cow eating asparagus and farting. Write NMDA in a gas bubble. Or print off a picture of a cow and a picture of some asparagus and a speech bubble, cut them out and make a collage yourself.

The physical activity of making this little collage will enter your episodic memory and also provide kinesthetic and visual reinforcement of the information. This sounds time-consuming, but it doesn't have to be. It's actually more time-efficient in the long run because you won't have to relearn the information.

4. Finally, it's time to learn the skeletal formula of NMDA.

Lucky for you that it looks like a cow! When you start creating memory boosters, you'll find that coincidences like this will happen more often, because you are priming your brain to look for patterns and find meaning. Now you can add more details to your collage (if your cow is facing to the left). Write HO next to the horn, write "OH dear!" next to the methane. The cow's udder might remind you of a hand (like a blown-up rubber glove), so hand = HaNd = HN. Doodle in the two Os and you have the structure.

This may all seem like a lot of effort to learn a few bits of information, but there is no easy way to learn. You can either stare at the page of facts and repeat them mindlessly to yourself until you are so bored you want to chew off your own arm (and then find you haven't actually retained anything), or you can have a little thinking adventure that is fun, feels a bit silly, and feels a bit as if you're wasting time (you're not—studying doesn't have to be dull and masochistic, you know).

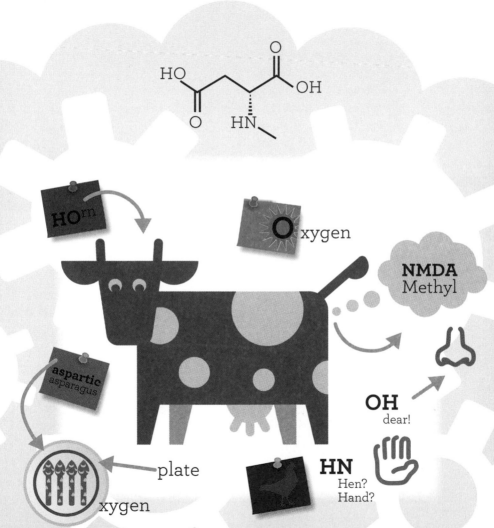

ASSOCIATION:
RELATE NEW INFORMATION TO EXISTING KNOWLEDGE

In the previous section, we saw how connecting new information to familiar imagery (e.g. cell phone, cow, asparagus) provides a hook on which to hang your new memories. This is because it is very difficult to learn anything without a context, and what you already know has a major impact on what you can learn. Your prior knowledge affects how you perceive new information.

To demonstrate this, here is a simple experiment. What is the first thing you think of when you see the word "FESTIVAL"? This will depend entirely on your upbringing, culture, and age. Some people will think of Christmas, others Diwali, Passover, Ramadan, birthdays, harvest, Newport, Woodstock. But the important thing is that you understand what a festival is without further explanation: it involves celebration, food, it is often associated with worship and commemoration, and it is usually fun, challenging, a test of faith, and a time for reflection. Now read this sentence:

"The festival of La Tomatina is held every year in the Valencian town of Buñol, Spain. The first event is the 'palo jabón,' when brave youths climb a greasy pole to reach a ham after which tomato battle commences with a cannon shot."

Because you have prior knowledge of festivals, you can understand the sentence and you can add this new information to your existing knowledge of festivals.

However, incorrect prior knowledge, or incorrect use of prior knowledge to give context, can also mislead. For example the phrase "battle commences with a cannon shot" would lead you to think that a weapon was used to start the tomato fight (since you associate cannons with battles in your memory); in fact a water cannon is used.

As you can see, prior knowledge has a huge impact on your future learning and how you make memories.

An analogy is a good example of this prior knowledge in action. In an earlier section, determining important meaning within a text was compared to mining for gold (see page 121). This analogy tapped into a shared understanding of the things most commonly associated with gold mining, namely that gold is precious and needs to be removed from the surrounding rock, which is hard work but potentially very rewarding. The inference was that key important facts are like precious nuggets of gold and digging them out of the text is necessary and potentially very rewarding, justifying the hard work and conscientious effort put in to acquire them.

So, when you are learning new information, use strategies to link and associate the material with your existing knowledge.

1. Consciously think back to situations in which you dealt with similar material. Ask yourself, "What is this like that I already know and understand?"

2. Briefly recap some key points from your prior knowledge to inform how you learn. For instance if you were learning about La Tomatina, you could research to find things in common with your own familiar festivals. So you might look to see what traditions, rules, and rituals are observed, or if there are any special costumes or pole decorations. This will guide how you search for information, and make it easier to learn.

3. Be aware that some of your prior knowledge can lead to incorrect assumptions about the new knowledge.

4. Always try to improve and deepen your understanding of ideas. View your ideas as testable, improvable objects.

5. Be curious; the more you let your curiosity flourish, the more connections and associations you will build as you research a new subject. For instance, aren't you curious about the total number of tomatoes used and who supplies them? This would lead you to discover that the estimated 150,000 tomatoes come all the way from Extremadura on the other side of the country, where they are grown specially for the festival (rather than for taste)...

WHILE WE TEACH,
WE LEARN

The benefits of teaching someone else have been known about for centuries: it was the Roman philosopher Seneca who said, "While we teach, we learn." Albert Einstein famously said, "If you can't explain it to a six-year-old, you don't understand it yourself," which is worth bearing in mind whenever you are tackling complex ideas. However, LDL ("Lernen durch Lehren" or "learning by teaching") has really only gained traction in modern teaching since the 1980s, when Jean-Pol Martin popularized it as a method of foreign language teaching in Germany.

Studies into LDL and "cascading mentoring" have found that when people have to teach a subject to someone else, they are more motivated to understand and learn the information themselves, plus the gaps and weaknesses in their understanding and knowledge are highlighted by trying to explain the concepts to a third party. LDL has also been found to improve self-esteem, self-confidence, and a sense of belonging.

One such 'cascading' mentoring program has recently been introduced at Penn Engineering, along with the Graduate School of Education, which has received a three-year, $600,000 grant from the National Science Foundation "to spur interest in computer science with a first-of-its-kind, 'cascading' mentoring program in which college, high school, and middle school students will learn with and from each other."

Undergraduates will teach and mentor high school and middle school students; the high school students will teach middle schoolers. "This learning-by-teaching approach will improve all of the students' understanding of computational thinking and purposes by exposure to a variety of hands-on software design activities and materials," said Susan Davidson, principal investigator and Chair of the Department of Computer and Information Science, University of Pennsylvania.

Computer scientists at Stanford and Vanderbilt universities are currently developing "Teachable Agents" called "The Betty's Brain System" which has been trialed with fifth grade science pupils. The children can teach the virtual agent to solve problems and the study found that "This motivates the students to learn more so they can teach their agent to perform better." The study also observed that "Beyond preparing to teach, actual teaching can tap into the three critical aspects of learning interactions—structuring, taking responsibility, and reflecting." So the children structured their learning more effectively, took responsibility to improve their own understanding, they reflected on how well they had taught the agent, and were more motivated to better prepare for future learning on related topics.

RESTRUCTURE AND REPOSITION
DIFFICULT INFORMATION

THE NINETEENTH-CENTURY GERMAN PSYCHOLOGIST HERMANN EBBINGHAUS, PIONEER IN THE EXPERIMENTAL STUDY OF MEMORY, DISCOVERED A LEARNING PHENOMENON WHICH HE CALLED THE "SERIAL POSITION EFFECT." HE OBSERVED THAT THE RECALL ACCURACY VARIES DEPENDING ON THE POSITION OF ITEMS WITHIN A LIST.

Spend one minute reading this list three times and trying to memorize all the items. Then write down as many as you can remember, before you continue reading:

circle, film, thermometer, album, vulture, rifle, gloves, signature, coffee, hammer, meteor, parachute

According to the serial position effect, you will remember more of the items at the beginning and end than those in the middle of the list. You also retain more information from the beginning and end of a study session than the middle.

That is why it's important to move information around, and vary the structure as you learn, so that you don't create the same memory blind spots. Flashcards (*see* page 138) are a great way to do this because you can shuffle them to change the order.

You must also work harder and pay more attention to difficult information, because your brain wants to take the path of least resistance; it wants to remember or recall the easy information and ignore the complicated information. This is called "availability heuristic" and we succumb to it all the time—interpreting the world around us based on immediate examples that spring to mind. However, basing judgments on the notion that, "if you can think of it, it must be important" is sloppy thinking that will often lead you astray.

ANSWER THIS QUESTION:

If you were to open a book at random and find the letter "K" in the text, which is more likely:

a) the word would start with a K;

b) K was the third letter?

The correct answer is b) but most people choose a) because several words spring to mind that start with K, but it is harder to think of words with K as their third letter. It's the same reason why people buy lottery tickets and overestimate the frequency of shark attacks or the danger of air travel.

People prefer data that is easy to obtain and they make decisions based on this limited information. Politicians know this, which is why they routinely quote dubious data and repeat sound bites to support their political arguments, because the electorate are all too eager to let themselves be spoonfed information rather than to engage their critical faculties and find out for themselves.

So, take the extra effort to learn the difficult material because otherwise you will shrink the world to fit your limited knowledge, when you should be motivated to increase your knowledge to understand its complexities.

Have you noticed how poorly educated people can speak with boorish certainty on matters about which they know very little? That's the availability heuristic, with an extra helping of "confirmation bias" (the tendency to favor information that confirms one's beliefs).

Consciously fighting against the availability heuristic will encourage you to be more rigorous in your learning:

- Be critical about your knowledge, ask yourself what specific observations are forming your belief, and examine reasons why you *shouldn't* believe it

- It is always better to spend time gathering data and researching than guessing or looking for material to support your limited knowledge

- Don't stop with an initial estimate; keep researching and looking for more information

CONSOLIDATION

CONSOLIDATION IS THE SINGLE MOST IMPORTANT MEMORY PRINCIPLE. MOST PEOPLE ARE FAMILIAR WITH IT, BUT STILL MANAGE TO IGNORE IT, FAVORING CRAMMING OR EXTENDED STUDY PERIODS OVER DISTRIBUTED LEARNING, WHEN THE LATTER IS LESS PAINFUL AND MORE EFFECTIVE.

The first recorded reference to the idea of memory consolidation appeared in the writings of the Roman teacher of rhetoric, Quintilian. He discussed the "curious fact... that the interval of a single night will greatly increase the strength of the memory," and observed that "the power of recollection... undergoes a process of ripening and maturing during the time which intervenes." The word "consolidation" was first applied to memory at the end of the nineteenth century by German researchers Georg Müller and Alfons Pilzecker, who conducted studies into the concept that memory needs time for "Konsolidierung."

Rehearsing or recalling information over spaced intervals reinforces neural pathways; synapses and the communication between brain cells become stronger the more frequently the same signal passes between them. If you doubt this, you have only to consider all the music you can hum and song lyrics you can recall without effort; you never sat down and learned them, you have simply heard them over and over again.

So you think you know all about consolidation. Did you know that caffeine enhances memory consolidation? In a recent study, published online in the journal *Nature Neuroscience*, 160 volunteers were shown 200 pictures of everyday items and asked questions about them. They were then given a pill containing 200 mg caffeine, or a placebo. In a memory test the next day, the caffeinated participants performed better than the control group. Senior author Michael A. Yassa, in an interview with *Medscape Medical News*, said, "My message from this study is that if, like me, you have a coffee habit, and drink several cups a day, this is another reason not to stop it."

TRY THE CAFFEINE MEMORY TEST

Spend three minutes memorizing these 25 objects. Tomorrow, take recall test number 1 on page 136 (no peeking). Then an hour later, look at page 135 and spend three minutes memorizing the other 25 objects. Then drink a cup of coffee and the day after tomorrow take recall test number 2 on page 137. Good luck—turn to the answers on page 144 to see what should have happened.

RECALL TEST NUMBER 1: WHICH OBJECTS ARE MISSING?

RECALL TEST NUMBER 2: WHICH OBJECTS ARE MISSING?

FLASHCARDS

You are probably familiar with flashcards but you may have overlooked them up to now as a learning and memory tool. They are a very powerful technique, but their simplicity and familiarity mean learners ignore them in favor of more novel and faddy studying methods.

Paper flashcards have been used since at least the early nineteenth century, when Favell Lee Mortimer, an English evangelical author of educational books for children, devised a set of phonics flashcards to teach children to read, called *Reading Disentangled,* in 1834.

Most flashcard systems rely on spaced repetition to consolidate information, as well as varying the length of review for cards for which the learning material appears to be secure, shortening it for material that is less secure. If you are a kinesthetic learner, you would benefit from making paper flashcards, but you can also create them digitally with apps like Quizlet, StudyBlue, Anki, and FlashCardMachine.

HOW TO MAKE AND USE FLASHCARDS

1. Your flashcards should be index cards about 4 x 6 inches (fold an 8½ x 11-inch sheet of paper in half vertically, then horizontally).

2. Write a question on one side.

3. Write your answer or answers on the other side.

4. Keep the content brief. Don't overcomplicate with hoards of information. Have only one term or concept per card. If the question asks for a list, try to keep the answer to a minimum of three items. If you need a longer list, split the question over two or more cards.

5. Color code your flashcards for different subjects.

6. Writing or typing the cards benefits tactile learners, and color-coding is good for visual learners. Just creating the cards helps you learn the material but don't spend so long creating them that you run out of time to perform memory games with them.

7. When the information is totally new, limit the number of cards to 50, otherwise you won't be able to go through all of them in one learning session.

8. Every time you start a new pile, shuffle the pack so that your learning remains independent from the order of the cards.

9. Read a question and write or recite your answer (writing is best because it's harder to cheat yourself into thinking you've given an adequate answer).

10. Look at the answer. If you are correct, place your card on the "correct" pile. If wrong, place on the "needs to study more" pile.

11. When you reach the end of the cards, pick up the "needs to study more" pile and go through them again.

12. Keep going until all your flashcards are on the "correct" pile.

LEITNER SYSTEM

This was devised by the German science journalist Sebastian Leitner in the 1970s. Keep the cards in five boxes labeled 1 to 5. In Box 1 keep the cards that you often get wrong and need to review. Keep in Box 5 the cards which you consider yourself to have securely learned.

Quiz yourself on the flashcards in Box 1 every day, Box 2 every 3 days, Box 3 every 5 days, Box 4 every week, and Box 5 once a month. Every time you get an answer right, promote the card to the next box.

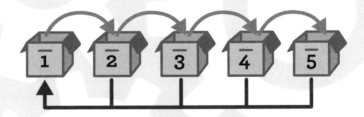

INCLUDE PICTURES IN YOUR ANSWERS

Studies show that pictures with words are more memorable than pictures alone. This is especially useful when using flashcards to learn foreign language vocabulary.

Congratulations, you have completed the first stage of your memory expanding adventure! If you have tried out all the puzzles and techniques, you will already be enjoying improved retention and recall, and more productive study. Now it's over to you. Using your new knowledge and regular daily practice, there's no limit to the incredible cognitive gains you can achieve.

BIBLIOGRAPHY

HOW THE BRAIN REMEMBERS

Bridge, Donna J., Paller, Ken A. "Neural Correlates of Reactivation and Retrieval-Induced Distortion." *The Journal of Neuroscience*, August 29, 2012.

MYTHS ABOUT MEMORY

Gamerman, Ellen. "The Brain Is Mightier Than the Camera When Remembering Art." *The Wall Street Journal*, December 17 2013.

YOU REMEMBER MORE THAN YOU THINK

Spock, Benjamin. *Baby and Child Care*. New York: Duell, Sloan and Pearce, 1946.

MEMORY ABILITY IS DEVELOPED, NOT INNATE

Chase, William and Simon, Herbert. "Perception in Chess." *Cognitive Psychology*, 1973.

SHORT-TERM MEMORY

Miller, George A. , "The Magical Number Seven, Plus or Minus Two: Some Limits on Our Capacity for Processing Information." *Psychological Review*, 1956 vol. 63, pp. 81-97.

TOPOGRAPHICAL MEMORY

Berthoz, Alain. *The Brain's Sense of Movement*. Cambridge: Harvard University Press, 2000.

DECLARATIVE MEMORY

Ogas, Ogi. "Who Wants to be a Cognitive Neuroscience Millionaire?" *Seed Magazine*, March 2014.

PROCEDURAL MEMORY

1. Gladwell, Malcolm. *Outliers: The Story of Success*. New York: Little, Brown and Company, 2008.
2. Colvin, Geoff. *Talent Is Overrated: What Really Separates World-Class Performers from Everybody Else*. Portfolio, 2008.

EMOTION AND MEMORY

Easterbrook, J. A. "The effect of emotion on cue utilization and the organization of behavior." *Psychological Review* 66 (3): 183–201, 1959.

EIDETIC MEMORY

Shafy, Samiha. "The Science of Memory: An Infinite Loop in the Brain." *Spiegel Online*, November 21, 2008.

MUSICAL MEMORY

1. Groussard, M., Viader, F., Hubert, V., Landeau, B., Abbas, A., Desgranges, B., Eustache, F., Platel, H. "Musical and verbal semantic memory: two distinct neural networks?" *NeuroImage*, Volume 49, Issue 3, February 1, 2010.
2. Janata, P. "The neural architecture of music-evoked autobiographical memories." *Cerebral Cortex*, 19, 2579-2594, 2009.
3. Macmillan, Jenny. "Successful Memorising." *Piano Professional*, September 2004.
4. Kageyama, Noa. "Does Mental Practice Work?" http://www.bulletproofmusician.com/does-mental-practice-work.
5. *Jan Lisiecki—The Reluctant Prodigy*. http://www.youtube.com/watch?v=vMMSLYZomXQ.

TALENT IS OVERRATED: DELIBERATE PRACTICE BRINGS SUCCESS

Ericsson, K., Prietula, M. J., Cokely, E. T. The Making of an Expert. *Harvard Business Review*, 85, 114-121, 2007.

LIVELY REPETITION VS. ROTE LEARNING

1. Herzberg, Frederick. "One More Time, How Do You Motivate Employees?" *Harvard Business Review*, 1968.
2. Pink, Daniel H. *Drive: The Surprising Truth About What Motivates Us*. New York: Penguin, 2009.
3. Chua, Amy. *Battle Hymn of the Tiger Mother*. New York: Penguin, 2011.

MUSCLE MEMORY AND MINDFUL PRACTICE

1. http:www.tomdowie.com/2014/01.
2. http:www.bulletproofmusician.com/david-kim-on-letting-go-and-being-yourself/#more-7815.
3. Powell, Michael. *Acting Techniques: An Introduction for Aspiring Actors*. Methuen Drama, 2010.
4. http://www.bettermovement.org/2012/merzenich-interview-on-neuroplasticity-and-the-feldenkrais-method.

CHUNKING AND PATTERNS

1. McCurry, Justin. "Chimps are making monkeys out of us." *The Observer*, September 29, 2013.
2. Bor, Daniel. *The Ravenous Brain: How the New Science of Consciousness Explains Our Insatiable Search for Meaning*. Basic Books, 2012.

OBJECT RECALL

McNamara, T.P., Rump, B., & Werner, S. "Egocentric and geocentric frames of reference in memory of large-scale space." *Psychonomic Bulletin and Review*, 10(3), 589-595, 2003.

HOW TO MINIMIZE MEMORY LOSS

Agrawal R., Gomez-Pinilla F. "'Metabolic syndrome' in the brain: deficiency in omega-3 fatty acid exacerbates dysfunctions in insulin receptor signalling and cognition." *Physiology*, May 15, 2012.

ATTENTION PLEASE

1. James, W. *The Principles of Psychology*. New York: Henry Holt, 1890.
2. Rosen, Larry. *iDisorder: Understanding Our Obsession with Technology and Overcoming Its Hold on Us*. New York: Palgrave Macmillan, 2012.

CONSOLIDATION

Borota, D., Murray, E., Keceli, G., Chang, A., Watabe, J. M., Ly, M., Toscano, J. P., Yassa, M. A. "Post-study caffeine administration enhances memory consolidation in humans." *Nature Neuroscience*, January 12, 2014.

ANSWERS

P8: HOW THE BRAIN REMEMBERS

Most people will get between five and-ten questions correct. If you got more than 12 correct, then well done indeed. This memory test is very challenging because we retain surprisingly little detail unless we are specifically looking for something (this shows how important attention is for forming memories).

Also, did you notice how easily you can be made to doubt your memories or create fake ones? How long did you spend wondering which animal was asleep on the armchair, or considering the position of non-existent apples and pairs of shoes? Did you name a key as one of your three metal objects in question 14 (immediately after reading the word "key" in question 13)?

In a week's time, take the test again and notice how your prior memory of the questions directs your attention. Naturally, you should perform much better this time, because now your attention is guided by your declarative memory (*see page 45*).

The other exercises in this section are to give you hands-on experience of some of the principles being explained (rather than give you a memory score), so don't despair if you found some of them tough. Use your scores as a benchmark to track your progress.

P26: YOU REMEMBER MORE THAN YOU THINK

The fourth image is the correct Madagascar.

P38: SENSORY MEMORY

The big tree in the middle is missing.

P47: SEMANTIC MEMORY

1. Apple
2. Red
3. a,d
4. Cyanidin
5. True

P48: DECLARATIVE MEMORY

1. Libra
2. South Korea
3. James Bond; climbing accident in the French Alps.
4. knee joint
5. Reginald Dwight
6. wind velocity
7. chocolate, vanilla, strawberry
8. Detective Comics
9. it knocked over a lantern
10. almond

P52: EMOTION AND MEMORY

1. Most people will notice yellow on the weapon as this is the brightest color and at the front of the weapon.
2. Most people will notice that the outfit was black but will not be able to give any further detail such as the shape of the necklace or that the makeup is pastel.
3. The ears have been removed! However, in the shock of looking at the picture you wouldn't focus on this otherwise very noticeable feature.

Most people will be able to give some detail to questions 1 and 2, but will totally miss the answer to question 3.

P80: CHUNKING AND PATTERNS

The nine squares of a tic-tac-toe board, going from top left to bottom right.

If you number each face of the Rubik's cube like this:
123
456
789
you can describe the positions of each color, so for example, left face, top face, right face

267	3	5	GREEN

so the answers for BLUE, WHITE, and YELLOW are:

3	18	9	BLUE
0	24	167	WHITE
18	5	3	YELLOW

The word DRAGON is an acronym (*see* page 103)
Dog
Rabbit
Anteater
Gorilla
Octopus
Newt

P92: MEMORY HOOK NUMBER RHYME
Top ten safest countries.

P95: MEMORY PEG ALPHABET
Most people should get over 20 using this method, which is considerably more than if you just used your normal non-associative recall.

P106: ACROSTICS
The initial letter of the lines spell Elizabeth.
Acrostic Passwords: Night Fever, I Walk the Line, In Da Club, Bohemian Rhapsody, Disturbia, Yellow, Do I Wanna Know?, London Calling, You Ain't Nothin' But a Hound Dog, Purple Rain, Halo, Space Oddity

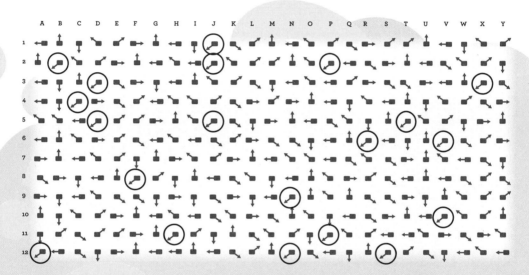

P118: ATTENTION PLEASE
 1J, 2B, 2J, 2P, 3D, 3X, 4C, 5D, 5J, 5T, 6R, 6V, 8F, 9N, 10V, 11H, 11P, 12A, 12N, 12S

You should be able to spot all 20 within two minutes with 100 percent accuracy. If you have made any mistakes, pick another icon and try again, only this time slow down and concentrate on accuracy instead of speed. Here are the coordinates for all the icons, so you can practice:

(42) 1B, 1G, 1M, 1U, 2A, 2F, 2N, 2T, 3C, 3I, 3W, 4O, 4T, 5H, 5N, 5S, 5Y, 6B, 6Q, 6U, 7B, 7G, 7L, 7U, 8E, 8I, 8O, 8U, 9O, 9Q, 9V, 10A, 10F, 10N, 10T, 10Y, 11G, 11K, 12F, 12I, 12M, 12R

(39) 1E, 1L, 1P, 1S, 1T, 1Y, 2D, 2L, 2M, 2X, 3K, 3Q, 4F, 4J, 4M, 4W, 5E, 5F, 5V, 6E, 6K, 6X, 7E, 7J, 8G, 8R, 8X, 9X, 9Y, 10D, 10X, 11B, 11D, 11E, 11I, 11N, 11R, 12L, 12T

(34) 1F, 1R, 2E, 2S, 3F, 3R, 3U, 4D, 4L, 4N, 4Y, 5G, 5M, 5X, 6D, 6L, 6Y, 7A, 7H, 7K, 7T, 8B, 8Q, 9A, 9H, 9K, 9T, 10E, 10L, 10S, 11F, 11V, 11X, 12E

(42) 1K, 1Q, 2R, 2V, 3E, 3L, 3S, 3T, 3Y, 4E, 4K, 4X, 5K, 5P, 6F, 6J, 6M, 6N, 6W, 7Q, 7S, 7X, 8A, 8K, 8S, 8W, 8Y, 9E, 9F, 9J, 9R, 9S, 10J, 10M, 10R, 11C, 11L, 1W, 12C, 12K, 120, 12U

(33) 1C, 1I, 1W, 2Y, 3B, 3G, 3M, 4B, 4Q, 4U, 5L, 5R, 5W, 6O, 6T, 7F, 7Y, 8C, 8H, 8M, 9B, 9G, 9I, 9L, 9U, 0B, 10P, 11A, 11J, 11O, 12D, 12Q, 12V

(48) 1A, 1H, 1N, 1V, 2G, 2I, 2Q, 2U, 3A, 3H, 3N, 3P, 3V, 4A, 4G, 4P, 4S, 5C, 5O, 6A, 6G, 6I, 6P, 6S, 7C, 7M, 7P, 7W, 8D, 8J, 8N, 8T, 8V, 9C, 9M, 10G, 10I, 10Q, 10U, 11S, 11T, 12B, 12G, 12H, 12J, 12P, 12W, 12Y

(42) 1D, 1O, 1X, 2C, 2H, 2K, 2O, 2W, 3J, 3O, 4H, 4I, 4R, 4V, 5A, 5B, 5I, 5Q, 5U, 6C, 6H, 7D, 7I, 7N, 7O, 7R, 7V, 8L, 8P, 9D, 9P, 9W, 10C, 10H, 10K, 10O, 10W, 11M, 11Q, 11U, 11Y, 12X

P123–P124: STRUCTURE AND ORGANIZE THE INFORMATION

1. It's easier to remember as: 0123456789 0123456789 0123456789
2. Five gold rings, four calling birds, three French hens, two turtle doves.
3. Imagine a cat stands on the window drinking from a saucer next to a vase of flowers. By the window a table is laid for dinner: knife, fork and spoon, cup and jug of water and a plate with a chicken leg, potato and carrots.

As with the research trials, the names or parts of the names in the harder or more unusual fonts should have been easier to recall. However, the font of one of the names is so hard to read that it may have hampered your encoding.
Daniel Oppenheimer: Daniel is written in Haettenschweiler font, which should have helped encoding. Oppenheimer is a famous name (J. Robert Oppenheimer was one of the "fathers of the atomic bomb") so that should have been the easiest surname to recall.

Connor Diemand-Yauman: The font for Diemand-Yauman makes it very hard to read, so this may have affected encoding, although if you had associated it with "Diamond" you would have encoded that part easily. According to the serial position effect, you will remember more of the items at the beginning and end than those in the middle of the list, so this name is the hardest of the three to recall.
Erikka Vaughan: The surname was written in Comic Sans Italicized font, and also came at the end of the list, so it should be more easily recalled.

P136: CONSOLIDATION
As with the study referred to on page 133, you should have a better recall of the images after the caffeine drink on the second recall test.